A Philosophy for Future Generations

Also available from Bloomsbury

A Short Philosophical Guide to the Fallacies of Love,
José A. Díez and Andrea Iacona
How to Think about the Climate Crisis, Graham Parkes
Morality and Ethics at War, Deane-Peter Baker
Politics in the Times of Indignation, Daniel Innerarity
The Philosophy and Art of Wang Guangyi, edited by Tiziana Andina and Erica Onnis
The Philosophy of Art: The Question of Definition, Tiziana Andina

A Philosophy for Future Generations

The Structure and Dynamics of Transgenerationality

Tiziana Andina
Translated by Antonella Emmi

BLOOMSBURY ACADEMIC
LONDON • NEW YORK • OXFORD • NEW DELHI • SYDNEY

BLOOMSBURY ACADEMIC
Bloomsbury Publishing Plc
50 Bedford Square, London, WC1B 3DP, UK
1385 Broadway, New York, NY 10018, USA
29 Earlsfort Terrace, Dublin 2, Ireland

BLOOMSBURY, BLOOMSBURY ACADEMIC and the Diana logo are trademarks of Bloomsbury Publishing Plc

First published in Great Britain 2022
This paperback edition published 2023

Copyright © Tiziana Andina 2022
English language translation © Antonella Emmi

Tiziana Andina has asserted her right under the Copyright, Designs and Patents Act, 1988, to be identified as Author of this work.

Cover image: Brain light / Alamy Stock Photo.

All rights reserved. No part of this publication may be reproduced or transmitted in any form or by any means, electronic or mechanical, including photocopying, recording, or any information storage or retrieval system, without prior permission in writing from the publishers.

Bloomsbury Publishing Plc does not have any control over, or responsibility for, any third-party websites referred to or in this book. All internet addresses given in this book were correct at the time of going to press. The author and publisher regret any inconvenience caused if addresses have changed or sites have ceased to exist, but can accept no responsibility for any such changes.

A catalogue record for this book is available from the British Library.

Library of Congress Cataloging-in-Publication Data
Names: Andina, Tiziana, author. | Emmi, Antonella, translator.
Title: A philosophy for future generations : the structure and dynamics of transgenerationality / Tiziana Andina ; translated by Antonella Emmi.
Other titles: Transgenerazionalità. English
Description: London ; New York : Bloomsbury Academic, 2022. | Includes bibliographical references and index.
Identifiers: LCCN 2021029674 (print) | LCCN 2021029675 (ebook) | ISBN 9781350229822 (hb) | ISBN 9781350229839 (epdf) | ISBN 9781350229846 (ebook)
Subjects: LCSH: Philosophical anthropology. | Generations. | Social sciences–Philosophy. | Sociology–Philosophy.
Classification: LCC BD450 .A478713 2022 (print) | LCC BD450 (ebook) | DDC 128–dc23
LC record available at https://lccn.loc.gov/2021029674
LC ebook record available at https://lccn.loc.gov/2021029675

ISBN: HB: 978-1-3502-2982-2
PB: 978-1-3502-2986-0
ePDF: 978-1-3502-2983-9
eBook: 978-1-3502-2984-6

Typeset by Integra Software Services Pvt. Ltd.

To find out more about our authors and books visit www.bloomsbury.com and sign up for our newsletters.

By foreseeing events, before they become pressing, effective remedies can be found; for if the medicine is not administered in time, the illness becomes incurable.

(Niccolò Machiavelli, *The Prince*)

A people always has the right to review, to reform, and to alter its Constitution. One generation cannot subject future generations to its laws.

(Constitutional Act of 24 June 1793, and Declaration of the Rights of Man and the Citizen)

Contents

List of Figures — viii

1 Transgenerationality — 1
2 Anthropology — 31
3 Metaphysics — 69
4 A Few Applications — 131

Notes — 159
Bibliography — 167
Index — 173

List of Figures

1	Primary transgenerationality: the parental relationship	72
2	Resident population trend in Italy: 1861–2011	139
3	Resident population trend in Italy: 2001–2017	140
4	Trend in the overall resident population in Italy (Italian and foreign nationals) at 1 January of every year from 1960 to 2017	140
5	Italy Debt/GDP % (1861–2015)	141
6	Trend in public expenditure, as a % of GDP, on public sector wages and salaries and on cash welfare benefits	141

1

Transgenerationality

'Why should we put ourselves out of our way for future generations; what have they ever done for us?'

The activity of thinking – as Hannah Arendt holds in *The Life of the Mind*[1] – encompasses the capacity to assess the consequences of our actions. That is to say, the actions we perform on a daily basis, at various levels, do not just have a purpose or a function but also result in consequences that can prove decisive in steering the future. Thinking, therefore, means taking responsibility as far as possible, and as best as possible, for those consequences.

This book seeks to outline a fundamental framework for a philosophy for future generations.[2] That is, a philosophy that revolves around the fact that societies, just like institutions, are built to endure in time and not just to occupy and defend a physical space. Spatiality has, on the whole, occupied philosophy in addressing the question of society much more than temporality has. That is something I believe we should think about. Various factors make it possible for a society to endure over time. One factor is the never-ending passage of generations, as each new generation comes to form part of a social fabric, a political model and an ethical framework that unfold over the course of history. Such a model conceals an underlying problem that is generally underestimated, namely new generations come to form part of social and political arrangements that have largely been designed by the generations that came before them. It is as though each generation had to jump onto a moving car – a car whose model they have not been able to choose and whose direction of travel was largely decided by others. And if the car should break down or run off the road, the drivers and passengers would have to repair it on the spot, adopting makeshift fixes to a vehicle they have inherited, one that was originally chosen without thinking too much of the fact that sooner or later it would have to change hands. As Alessandro Ferrara puts it,

> A social order lasts over time and reproduces itself over the generations. It is a set of stable and interconnected normative expectations to which every new member of a society is somehow, with varying degree of success, *socialized*. While such 'order' represents the moment of continuity in social life and the moment that allows us to identify a given society as *that* specific society, we should also account for its transformation over time. Why and how does it change?[3]

That is pretty much the scenario we find ourselves in today, one that lies behind some of the major crises that Western democracies have repeatedly been facing for decades now. Such a scenario is characterized by its negligence towards the future, which is very neatly captured by a quip Woody Allen takes from Groucho Marx, expressing a doubt that slumbers in each and every one of us: 'Why should we put ourselves out of our way for future generations; what have they ever done for us?' Let us call this the common-sense argument. In general, the answer we give in perfectly good faith to that question is more or less,

> There's no reason why. Future generations don't exist and they don't feel pleasure or suffer pain. Instead, we who live in the here and now do, in various ways and in a multitude of circumstances, so it's absolutely legitimate to concern ourselves exclusively with the present, or at most the immediate future. For all the rest, only time will tell.

Such a reply conceals a gross neglect of our duty to steer the future. Given that social systems have an intrinsic diachronic structure, meaning they are designed to survive over time, neglecting that aspect can carry extremely high costs that emerge, covertly, with time.

The purpose of this book is to investigate the diachronic structure of societies. What does it mean for a society to endure over time? What does the passage of generations imply for a social system? What bond exists – if any – between generations? What are we talking about exactly when we talk of future generations? What kinds of problems emerge when we underestimate the diachronic structure of societies and when we underestimate the intergenerational relationship? In this book, I will argue that the diachronic dimension of societies is just as important as their synchronic dimension. In practice, if philosophers and social scientists do not turn their attention to understanding what structures govern the possibility for societies to endure in time, we have no hope of understanding society itself or its malfunctions. As such, I believe it is important to equip our social ontologies with a theoretical apparatus enabling us to understand the propensity of societies to extend in time through the generational bond. To do so, I will introduce the concept of transgenerationality, considering both the biological bond that unites generations (the biological transgenerational bond) and the bond that unites the passage of generations from a historical point of view. Then I will look at a particular type of social action – transgenerational social action – that is distinctive by virtue of its specific structure, which implies necessary cooperation between different generations to be effectively accomplished. As necessary as such cooperation is for all intents and purposes, it is not, however, equal, in the sense that while, on the one hand, we have a generation that decides what to do and how to do it, passing on the task of carrying on the action and bringing it to term to new generations, on the other, those new generations are simply asked to carry on the process and complete it as required, thus bearing the burden without having participated in the original decision-making process and, hence, without having ever consented to anything.

As we will see, both the transgenerational bond and transgenerational social actions make broad reference to the concept of future generations. The concept, however, is problematic in many ways. For instance, future generations do not exist, so technically they cannot be considered to have rights or duties, as quite clearly there is nobody to whom rights and duties can be attributed. Yet, the concept is absolutely fundamental for the success of transgenerational actions, as without future generations, transgenerational actions quite literally cannot exist. Thus, I will attempt to outline a metaphysical framework to understand the concept of future generations. In other words, I will try to answer the question of the identity of future generations. No social philosophy or political philosophy or social ontology can be developed, I believe, without clarifying what conception of the human being gives us our horizon. Thus, ample space will be dedicated to framing our discourse in a philosophical anthropology that forms both the foundation and the condition of possibility for a philosophy of future generations. Finally, the last chapter explores three examples that illustrate in practice the implications of addressing or ignoring the transgenerational issue. Specifically, I will discuss a historical example – the rise and fall of the Venetian Republic – and two exemplary cases characterizing our own times – pensions and climate change.

Self-preservation and growth: The law of the living

The aim of humankind is, as a norm, self-preservation and the growth of its vital energy. In general, that means that humans strive to enhance their being (in the individual and social dimensions) by using the methods available to them, which they have managed to develop over the course of history. Of particular significance in this regard is an article published in 1968 by the US biologist Garrett Hardin in the journal *Science*.[4] Attracting widespread acclaim from the scientific community, in the article Hardin addressed the issue of world population growth, arguing that there was a real risk that exponential growth in the population could not be matched by sufficient growth in food supply. What is certain for Hardin, in short, is that the problem of population growth is one that cannot be solved from merely a technical perspective, and so he proposes that the issue should be addressed from the broader horizon offered by a moral perspective.

Why was Hardin so pessimistic? Hardin describes the world as a closed system, containing a finite amount of resources. If the population in such a system grows exponentially, the result will be that as the population increases, there will be a corresponding decrease in resources, and the overall level of wealth will fall. Hardin's argument is based on the clear and ultimately simple assumption that the system is closed, therefore, it cannot expand beyond a certain point, which means in the long run it will be exhausted. Ours is a finite world, states Hardin in his starting hypothesis, and it should be treated as such. That picture ultimately offers a rather grim outlook for the destiny of humankind. To avoid the worst outcome, the solution, it would seem, is for the variables to be kept under control, placing limits, for instance, on world population growth. According to Hardin, however, that is rather unlikely to happen, for two reasons. The first is of a technical-mathematical nature. The second, the one of most interest for our purposes here, relates to anthropology and is more subtle in nature.

What Hardin refers to is known as the 'tragedy of the commons', which he derives from the moral tradition of Jeremy Bentham. Let us consider a scenario. Imagine living in a country before the advent of private property. Pastureland is not fenced off; the seas are not divided up. In such a condition of extreme freedom, the herdsmen let their cattle roam and graze freely, and in that way the interplay of the needs of the cattle and the production of pasture keeps the situation in a sort of natural equilibrium. In other words, the cycle of nature is such that the mortality of humans and cattle enables the natural reserves that provide nourishment to the cattle to regenerate spontaneously. Both biology and a highly respectable current of thought in philosophical tradition teach us that humans generally seek their own gain, first in terms of self-preservation and then in terms of growth. The theory is one of venerable age, dating back at least to seventeenth-century philosophy. It can be found, for instance, in the philosophy of nature that unites Spinoza and Nietzsche,[5] and its immediate theoretical foundations can be located in the concepts of *conatus* and the 'will to power'. In that framework, beings have a natural impulse for self-preservation, as Spinoza theorized, together with a natural impulse for self-preservation and growth, as Nietzsche saw it. We shall call this idea the 'preservation-growth' principle.

Given these premises, Hardin's theory is quite simple and consistent with the preservation-growth principle transferred to the biological and economic plane. Here is how the argument unfolds. Let us suppose that our herdsmen are all rational individuals and therefore are driven not only to seek their self-preservation and pursue their own individual good but also to maximize it. Thus, the scenario is one in which each herdsman works towards his own self-preservation by pursuing his own gain. Such a strategy, as we will soon see, is certainly an excellent one for the individual, but on the whole, that is, for all the herdsmen who live off the same land, and for the land itself and for future generations, it will be highly problematic. Each herdsman, therefore, will tend to consolidate the practices that enable his self-preservation and the maximization of his own gain, which in practice means he will attempt to take out to pasture as many head of cattle as possible. His gain, in fact, depends precisely on that, namely, on his use of the cattle and the intensification of that use. For the strategy to deliver the outcomes the herdsman seeks, however, it is clear that the natural resource will need to be used intensively, in such a way that will rapidly lead to its exhaustion.

The theoretically sensitive point for Hardin is precisely that, by striving for self-preservation, each human being tends to pursue his own gain. In doing so, he will pursue actions that are destructive for the very environment that provides him with the means and resources to maximize his own gain. For instance, he will take out to pasture on the commons as many head of cattle as possible, on the implicit assumption that 'the other herdsmen will choose their own gain. So if I don't do the same, I'll end up suffering an economic loss.' Hence, a society that believes in and intends to apply broad-scale, free access to commons will be destined in the long run to promote its own destruction. Alongside that, Hardin stresses the importance of a second point, specifically, our natural dispositions conflict with the limits of the ecosystem in which we live. That fact is a permanent one, given that it flows from a natural disposition. As such, to prevent the collapse of the system, corrective action needs to be taken through education, even though over successive generations such efforts will be nullified.

Thus, Hardin turns the point on its head, as it is biology that appears to determine the space of possibilities for the construction of culture. Given that the overriding objective of nature is the self-preservation and growth of living beings, human beings will obviously, more or less consciously, steer their individual, social and political lives towards that objective. Like it or not, there is a reverse side to the coin. The self-preservation-growth principle appears difficult to reconcile with the fact that the physical-environmental world, just like social institutions, is meant to last for a much longer time than the lifetime reserved for people.

Let us look at exactly what that means and what the implications are for our social structures.

From immortality to endurance: Biology and society

It is best to bear in mind that we are not immortal. The question of the endurance of our social structures and institutions is an important matter, one linked to how and why we exist in the world. In other words, given the fact that immortality is not within our reach in the medium term,[6] and may not even be all that desirable, what human beings can reasonably do instead is pursue the goal of building stable social structures and arrangements with effective normative power, as the preservation of such power will enable society as a whole to pursue longer-term objectives of broader scope. Which, ultimately, is what characterizes the human condition. Thus, it has proven particularly important to construct sophisticated social entities, such as institutions, states, metastates, and aggregations of states, which delegate a part of their powers to a supranational body in an effort to establish much broader and, ideally, much tighter-knit institutions. The duration of social structures of this kind cannot be taken for granted – they can last a long time, even a considerable period of time, but only providing certain necessary conditions are respected for such social institutions to survive. And, as demonstrated later through three examples, that cannot be taken for granted. The underlying idea, as anticipated, is that besides the normative structures that all societies create to enable rules to be enforced, there is a bond – the transgenerational bond – that emerges in a particular kind of social action – transgenerational social action – which makes it possible for our social structures to extend in time.

Thus, to begin with, the focus will be on locating where transgenerationality emerges, before investigating its origin and structures. Initially, an assumption will be made that there are two levels on which transgenerationality emerges. The first, as highlighted by psychologists, is the biological transgenerationality that emerges in the shadows of trauma. The second, which directly concerns, instead, philosophers and social ontologists, consists of the transgenerationality that unites the historical passage of the generations, and which emerges in certain social actions we call transgenerational social actions.

Primary transgenerationality: Traces and trauma

'A generation goes and a generation comes / yet the earth remains as ever.'[7]

The story of Antigone is one that strikes deep at the heart of who we are as human beings. Hegel interprets the story as a symbolic tale of the conflict between the social dimension of life, tied to the most basic and primitive of emotions, and the political dimension of civic and political power. Of the ancient myths, *Antigone* arguably offers the best insight for understanding the biological structure of the transgenerational bond and how it emerges in family relationships. The story of Antigone is the well-known story of a family swept and shaken by tragic events almost too devastating to mention. Indeed, it is the protagonist's sister, Ismene, who recalls the entire affair to a grieving Antigone, wracked with pain and anger over a law decreed by Creon, the king. That law forbids the burial of one of the two sisters' brothers. Before the battle between Eteocles and Polynices, two brothers destined to govern Thebes on alternate years, the story of that family had witnessed both parricide and incest, for a guiltless yet guilty Oedipus had killed his father – in the guise of a beggar encountered by chance on the road – and then married a women he did not know to be his mother. That series of events would determine the misfortunes of the city of Thebes, hit by a devastating plague, and of the two brothers, Eteocles and Polynices, who would both die in the battle waged between them. It is at this point that Antigone's tragedy begins. A tragedy that captures and conveys the sense of the often irreconcilable conflict between the law of the heart and the law of the state, all the more so because the young woman feels compelled to bear on her shoulders, like a second skin, that constellation of family misfortunes which Oedipus unwittingly set in motion, and which the two brothers would end, bringing to fruition a family saga steeped in tragedy. Antigone, unlike her sister Ismene, refuses to shrink from her family bonds, from their burden and their ties. To that web of bonds, suffering and tragedy, she shows complete loyalty. Antigone takes entirely upon herself the value and meaning of those bonds and chooses to act accordingly, also on the social level. By doing so, she protects the bond that ties her family together and to her.

It can happen, however, that the family bond is severed, violated or betrayed. But even in such cases, the presence of the transgenerational bond, and the duties that give it perceptible form, emerges clearly, precisely because it is absent. In particular, it becomes evident in trauma, in circumstances where something goes wrong and the bond becomes problematic or opaque. The transgenerational bond between blood relations or within family relationships is generally taken for granted, and for good reason. What is interesting on the theoretical plane instead is the question of whether a transgenerational bond is possible outside blood relations. How can a certain generation, for instance, feel guilt for the massacres of war perpetrated by generations past?[8] How can the Afro-American community still today suffer the traumas experienced over three hundred years – and many generations – ago by its forbears? Why do those traumas still persist and resist being overcome, giving rise to a psychological suffering that takes the form of social revolt?

Psychologists and philosophers have addressed this matter extensively, building theories that entail demanding ontological commitments. Among the concepts they have introduced are the collective psyche, the collective unconscious[9] and collective intentionality – three terms that have enjoyed extraordinary success, coined respectively by three illustrious intellectuals: Sigmund Freud, Ernst Jung and John Searle. Freud introduced the notion of a collective psyche as an extension of the individual psyche, mirroring the way the latter works. He argued, in particular, that it is the sense of guilt for an action which has been passed down for generations that reveals the existence of the collective psyche.[10] Jung instead theorized the existence of a collective unconscious, which he based on the idea of synchronicity, that is, the meaningful coincidence of two causally unrelated events for the individual. For Jung, the collective unconscious is understood as a sort of unconscious that is shared and shaped collectively, and which causally affects our development, making us who and what we are. It is what permits the accumulation, formation and transmission of human experience from generation to generation; it is innate and, therefore, universal.[11]

Finally, the American philosopher John Searle introduced the theory of collective intentionality as the specific capacity of the mind that disposes us as human beings to conceive of ourselves in the plural. Such a disposition, he argues, is primitive and, hence, has biological bases, which steers human action in a collaborative sense, bringing humans to take on a plural identity. Thus, Searle turns the common-sense assumption on its head, laying the groundwork for a non-conventional philosophical anthropology in which humans have a natural disposition for sociality and are only accidentally individualistic.[12] All these theories – the collective psyche, the collective unconscious and collective intentionality – aim to answer questions that are ultimately quite simple: how does the biological bond that ties parents and children (or that constitutes, in any case, the fundamental bond underpinning the family as a primary social structure) transfer to the most complex of social structures, of which the biological bond is just one component?

'Invisible loyalties' compel us to pay the debts of our ancestors, writes Anne Schützenberger,[13] who has dedicated much time and energy to studying biological and psychological transgenerational transfer, or what I call 'primary transgenerationality'. However, while the structure of primary transgenerationality appears fairly self-evident (notwithstanding the mysteries yet to be explored, mostly concerning the dynamics of the psyche), the structures and dynamics of secondary transgenerationality – the social bond that marks the passage of generations – are much less intuitive, as they are often connected with surplus ontological commitments, such as, for example, the introduction of entities that are both invisible and difficult to justify from a theoretical point of view. Searle's theory of collective intentionality attempts to overcome that sort of objection by specifying that it does not require the postulation of some sort of Hegelian world spirit or the existence of a super mind. Rather, it is an innate disposition that enables us to conceptualize the world from the 'we' rather than the 'I' point of view.[14] Thus it does not imply the idea of the existence of an extended mind or unconscious, but rather considers the disposition to think in terms of 'us' rather than 'me' as natural and logically prior, stressing how such a disposition does not require construction because it is, to wit, biologically innate. Searle, therefore, does not duplicate entities, but instead highlights the need to rethink the classical conception of intentionality. Thus, it is the plural dimension that characterizes human beings, which by extension, helps explain how transgenerational transfers occur.[15] The priority of the 'we' over the 'I' would suggest that our plural identity is prior to our individual identity, for which our disposition to think of ourselves as collective entities is what, ultimately, steers our actions. Moreover, collective intentionality determines and, where necessary, modifies the content of individual intentionality.

As we can see, while Searle's theory promises less of an ontological commitment, it calls into question consolidated theories held equally by philosophical anthropology and psychology, which generally consider the formation of individuality as one of the first tasks that humans perform in their growth process. Indeed, from the human disposition for cooperation, which we can easily introduce as a theoretical option, it does not follow that the 'we' has logical priority over the 'I'. As such, I would like to try introducing two working hypotheses. The first is the idea that for primary transgenerationality to exist, and be effective, it need not require assumptions that entail demanding ontological commitments, such as the existence of a super mind or an extended unconscious, or the introduction of hypotheses that overturn the established truths of the most consolidated traditions of philosophical anthropology. As with all other animals, humans possess instinctual dispositions that drive us first and foremost to self-preservation. That instinct is what characterizes the individual dimension. Nevertheless, having said that, it must be reiterated how transgenerational relationships are self-evident in a range of rather complex circumstances, from the transmission of trauma, as an exemplary case, to the formation of public debt, which concern both the biological sphere (primary transgenerationality) and the cultural sphere (secondary transgenerationality).[16]

To identify the conditions of possibility for both primary and secondary transgenerationality, it will be useful to consider the concept of the trace. Schützenberger insists repeatedly throughout her book on two points. Firstly, on the existence of transgenerationality, which she has observed in various ways and with various traits throughout the course of her career as a psychologist in her clinical and therapy work. Secondly, on the difficulty of identifying the mechanisms that govern transgenerational transmission. Thus, she introduces the idea of an extended unconscious, something which is both a bridge and a reservoir of all that a mother and father pass on to a child, and that one generation passes on to the next. What the structure and mechanisms of the extended unconscious are is obviously a complex matter, and Schützenberger is unable to say much in that regard. What she prefers to do instead, with an abundance of detail and rhetorical effect, is to describe episodes in which transgenerational transfer appears evidently at work. Those episodes include some that are particularly loaded with emotional and symbolic complexity, such as cases of families where a son dies and the little brother born after clearly carries the signs of that death, as though he were literally the ghost of his deceased brother. Vincent van Gogh and Salvador Dalì are two such examples. The phenomenon is known as the 'replacement child' syndrome,[17] where a baby is conceived to replace the loss of another child, often carries the name of the deceased sibling and may even be born on the anniversary of the death, where, in Schützenberger's view, the rituality of burial and the symbolic laying to rest of the deceased child has not been brought to completion. When that happens, the life of the 'replacement child' is generally not the happiest.

It was, for instance, the destiny of Vincent van Gogh, born on 30 March 1852, one year and one day after the death of his older brother, Vincent. The family spoke little of the death of the first Vincent; however, the second Vincent, the painter, was given both names of his dead sibling, Vincent-Wilhelm. The poor Vincent's destiny would be a tragic one. When he received a letter from one of his brothers, Theo, announcing the birth of a son who would similarly be named, out of affection, Vincent-Wilhelm, Vincent the painter attempted suicide. Theo hoped that his son Vincent-Wilhelm would live to achieve great things. But for Vincent, there were too many Vincents crowding his world with uncomfortable presences. Salvador Dalì experienced a similar situation to Van Gogh. In contrast, however, he learned to speak about it and adopt a psychological strategy that would enable him to defend himself from the crushing weight of the loss of his brother. Salvador had an elder brother whose same name he bore and for whom he was, in a way, a replacement. The 'real' Salvador was the brother whose tomb his mother would visit and weep over twice a week. The artist therefore decided to transform himself into a clown to distinguish himself from that brother. The words by which Dalì retold that part of his life are significant:

> I experienced death before living life … My brother died […] three years before I was born. His death plunged my father and my mother into the depth of despair … And in my mother's belly, I already felt their [my parents'] anguish. My fetus swam in a hellish placenta. I felt deep the persistence of this presence—a kind of theft of affection … This dead brother whose ghost welcomed me … it is not by chance that he was named Salvador, like my father and like me … I learned to live by filling up the gap of the affection which was not really given to me.[18]

Curiously, Schützenberger does not examine the explanation sketched out by Dalì, who was convinced that his environment influenced him profoundly, from as early as when he, or rather the foetus that would evolve into him, was in his mother's 'hellish' womb, imbued with the sense of death that had eaten up his parents after his brother's death. For Dalì, the sense of death that hung all around him would appear, in some way, to be the ghost of the brother, welcoming him to the world. There is no need to appeal to notions such as a collective mind or extended unconscious to explain that sense of annihilation. It is sufficient to assume that the young Salvador grasped the traces of his brother's death in the salient aspects of the environment that surrounded him in his early infancy. Those traces left their mark deeply on him, but he reacted with strength and creativity. It is reasonable to suppose that the bond, the combined outcome of the young Dalí's sensibility and the traces left in the environment by the painter's parents, generated that sense of loss and mourning. The transgenerational transfer would have been conveyed in part directly by the parental relationship and in part by the environment that provided the setting for that relationship, in which traces dense with meaning had been left.

That, at least, is what the American cartoonist Art Spiegelman suggests in his graphic novel *Maus*, which reconstructs his sense of being a replacement child, a brother replacing a brother. *Maus* is dedicated to his brother Richieu and to his mother. A photograph of Richieu opens the second volume of the story, in which the Jews are represented by mice and the Nazis by cats and pigs. From an exchange between Spiegelman and his wife, we learn that the photograph was for Spiegelman the most tangible object he had to revisit the memory of his brother:

'My Ghost-Brother, since he got killed before I was born. He was only five or six. After the war my parents traced down the vaguest rumors, and went to orphanages all over Europe. They couldn't believe he was dead. I didn't think about him much when I was growing up ... he was mainly a large, blurry photograph hanging in my parents' bedroom.'

'Uh-huh. I thought that was a picture of you, though it didn't *look* like you.'

'That's the point. They didn't need photos of me in their room. I was *alive!* ... The photo never threw tantrums or got into any kind of trouble ... It was an ideal kid, and *I* was a pain in the ass. I couldn't compete. They didn't talk about Richieu, but that photo was a kind of reproach. *He'*d have become a *doctor* and married a wealthy Jewish girl ... the creep. But at least we could've made *him* deal with Vladek. It's *spooky*, having sibling rivalry with a snapshot! I never felt guilty about Richieu. But I did have nightmares about S.S. men coming into my class and dragging all us Jewish kids away.[19]

Even here, we have a person who feels he has a ghost brother, one born before him, to whom he feels closely tied. In Spiegelman's story, the loss of a son was a highly traumatic experience for the parents, who were unable to cope with the grieving process. As little as they spoke of him, Richieu was ever present, and the parents' silence went hand in hand with an idealization process that led the young Spiegelman to feel an irremediable distance between himself and his brother. The same distance that separates the real from the ideal. In all these cases, primary transgenerationality conveys the sense of suffering and loss, transmitting painful emotions that, in the most dramatic circumstances, prevents independent identity from being formed.

Provisionally, it can be said that primary transgenerationality is like a web of relationships that leaves traces. Such traces have specific causes – a repressed suffering, stifled tears, a prolonged silence dense with words left unsaid. Whenever all this is the case, transgenerational transfer will revolve around trauma, pain and loss, and bear what is a visible absence. It is interesting to note how such a process can occur not just within close family circles. D.S.W. Leon Anisfeld and Arnold D. Richards have observed how something very similar happens around the margins of collective tragedies of Holocaust proportions: 'A child born to Holocaust survivors replaces not simply a specific dead child or ancestor, but all those who have perished.'[20] Entire generations can mourn the loss of the victims of a tragedy, even if they never knew any of the dead. That sense of loss and grief is conveyed by the emotions of parents or of those who experienced the tragedy first-hand, and it is internalized in the form of a vast array of negative emotions, including sadness, grief, anguish, hyper-alertness and uncontrolled anger, to name just a few.

Secondary transgenerationality: Locating the emergency in society

Let us now turn to secondary transgenerationality (or social transgenerationality), in an attempt to outline its key characteristics.

To begin with I will provide three examples exploring the application of transgenerationality, to which I will return in greater depth in the final chapter. The first example comes from the economic sphere. The global financial crisis that hit Western economies at length as of 2007 to 2008 was a particularly serious economic crisis, which especially impacted national states, provoking a sovereign debt crisis. The crisis emerged most clearly and dramatically in countries most exposed through high public debt levels and weak economic growth. That proved the case for countries in the southern Mediterranean area. However, it is well known that similar problems could emerge in even the most solid economies, such as the United States, in the event of weakening economic growth. I shall call this the question of 'contracting public debt'. In everyday life, we are generally quite careful when it comes to contracting debts, whether tangible or intangible in nature. The reason is quite simple. Debts have to be repaid – it is something we all know, something we are all taught. Indeed, for Plato it was a question of justice, which he defines, albeit provisionally, as: 'paying back what one has received'.[21] Similarly, the Latin phrase *unicuique suum* – 'to each his own' – is well known to have been one of the main precepts of Roman law. The underlying principle, therefore, is that it is only fair – imperative even – to return what is lent to us. In general, it is a precept that nobody ever questions, and which revolves around the idea that there are things or rights that belong to the sphere of individual property, of which we can never be deprived – unless of course we consent to it, such as by waiving the debt – or of which if we are deprived, then some sort of compensation must necessarily be offered. Plato gave a series of extremely practical examples, presenting the problem of 'returning' as one primarily tied to the availability of tangible things. In reality, there are no such particular limits, if not in terms of immediacy and presence, which lead us to privilege the return of things with physical consistency, be they a field, a house or a million euros. Presumably, we should be more alert to the issue when it is a matter of protecting intangible things or collective goods, to which we are particularly exposed – as is precisely the case with the formation of public debt, understood in the general sense of debt contracted by the state, state-owned enterprises or government bodies and entities.

The question is an interesting one, as it concerns both the mechanisms for contracting debt and how it is repaid. Long-term public debt is contracted to pay for expenditures which are not covered by the ordinary economic resources available to a state. Public debt is recorded in the balance of payments in the capital account, while interest paid to service the debt is recorded in the current account. These days, nearly all states need to contract public debt, especially in situations where there are extraordinary expenditures to be covered that exceed ordinary revenues, and for which the government does not intend to introduce new forms of taxation, sell state assets or issue new currency. There can be very good reasons to prefer debt formation to any of those alternative options. For instance, a government may not want to raise inflation by printing money, or it may prefer not to sell off any state assets, no matter how small a part, or it may believe that the tax burden is already sufficiently high and cannot be raised any further. Such options, moreover, are generally short-term measures and bode no good for the popularity of governments, which in contrast to states, have short lifespans and are formed by election. Quite simply, that means they need the approval of voters.

Thus, the mechanism that leads governments to contract public debt resolves short-term problems, while creating others in the longer term. In practice, what happens is that the mechanism shifts public finance problems forward in time, something that is of particular benefit to the government adopting the solution (which is generally implemented in the short term) but less so for the state, which will have to deal with the implications in the medium to long term. In this framework, and consistently with philosophical anthropology, individuals and governments work first and foremost to promote their self-preservation and power, and so they have a tendency to largely neglect the future, which in any case is not their main goal. Nevertheless, the future counts – in the non-negligible sense at least – as long-term debt will have to be paid by people who did not contract the debt; that is, by future generations that had no say whatsoever in the formation of the debt and that never agreed to contribute to paying off the debt.[22] If those future generations were to refuse to honour the agreements made by the state and their obligations, the risk of major political strife would be high – if not tragic, as the events that led to the outbreak of the Second World War (to choose one of the more striking examples) serve to show.

I will return to this matter further on, as it is one of major importance and clearly highlights the unavoidable necessity of transgenerationality. Given the structure of our societies, which depend on human beings for their formation, but which once formed are independent of them, it clearly emerges how the transgenerational bond is fundamental for the survival of complex societies over time, as actions that require a long time span to be completed demand the cooperation of the generations that come after the generation which originally chose to undertake the action. Let us now look at a second example, drawn from questions tied to climate change and sustainable development. The scientific literature abounds with statistics and commentary on this point. The anthropogenic nature of climate change is a well-established certainty supported by robust research.[23] The issue posed by the harmful changes shaping the climate and its evolution is patently of a transgenerational nature, in that it concerns in a stable way the relationship between generations. It would appear founded and fair to assert that every generation is obliged to leave the planet, ideally at least, in the same conditions as it found it, in what is known as the 'equality model'. The 'equality model', as Edith Brown Weiss notes,[24] lies midway between two more radical theories. At one end she identifies the 'opulence model', according to which there is no reason for people today to forgo or sacrifice benefits, given that their well-being is and remains a primary objective. At the other end there is the 'preservationist model', which stresses the need to preserve natural resources as much as possible so as not to deplete those resources, which do not belong to us but should instead be considered common goods. Midway, as mentioned, lies the equality model. Supporters of the latter position claim that an obligation exists which ties us to the future and which is expressed as a minimum collective commitment, which should be acknowledged in law, to leaving the planet in 'at least' the same conditions in which our generation found it. That obligation rests on at least two assumptions. First, since our planet is a common good, in theory it should be available not just to one generation at time x but also to future generations to come. Second, since many of the planet's resources are considered a good in and of themselves, as such they should be preserved. For example, water resources.

The theory that some kind of environmental protection is necessary is often paired with the theory that a sustainable development model is likewise needed. And the idea of sustainable development is a matter that similarly concerns transgenerationality. The World Commission on Environment and Development (WCED) defines sustainable development as 'development that meets the needs of the present without compromising the ability of future generations to meet their own needs'.[25] Both those theories – as to the need to preserve the environment at the minimum levels at least described by the equality model, and as to the need to introduce a sustainable development model to be able to achieve that – would in principle appear to follow from the largely non-controversial argument that while our societies should continue to pursue growth and wealth, such growth and wealth cannot imply unsustainable costs for future generations, that is, for those who will inhabit the planet after us. Looking more closely at the details of the various elements at play, however, it is easy to see how what seems to make plain common sense – environmental protection – in reality conceals a complexity of issues calling for more systematic thinking. For instance, the axiom of the intergenerational relationship becomes somewhat more complicated when approached from the perspective of law. Legal thinkers would typically be perplexed by any proposal to grant rights and attribute duties to people who do not exist. Then there is debate around what kind of obligation can be imposed on present generations to the benefit of future generations. On the other hand, if such an obligation were justified, there is the question of how institutions could be tasked to enforce it.

Generally speaking, those who oppose the idea of granting rights to future generations and, therefore, imposing obligations on present generations base their argument on the simple intuition that rights cannot be granted to people who do not exist, precisely because they do not exist. Persons who do not exist, just like generations that do not exist, are nothing, hence they cannot even demand the acknowledgement of certain rights.[26] The question is a particularly delicate one also because it is not those persons, and those generations, who demand acknowledgement of certain rights. It is other people and other generations who are doing so in their stead and for their benefit, as such. Providing, of course, that it is effectively a benefit. In this regard, Derek Parfit has formulated a paradox that is worth considering closely,[27] which rests on the assumption that it is highly likely that future births will be strictly correlated to changes in the environment.[28] Let us suppose that a state decides to introduce laws requiring certain measures to be taken on the environmental front, measures concerning urban transport, let us say, which is known to cause high levels of pollution. Let us also suppose that the measures effectively manage to cut air pollution levels significantly, especially in the short term, bearing a significant impact in the first decade following their adoption. It is known that there is a dependent relationship between deteriorating environmental conditions and new births, such that a substantial change in the environment will end up determining the birth of certain individuals rather than others. Therefore – and herein lies the paradox – a community that decides to address the environmental issue of pollution by not aggravating the state of the environment in which it lives to the benefit of the quality of life of future generations, as the equality model suggests, paradoxically will end up harming precisely those individuals it wants, in theory, to protect. That is because a change in environmental conditions, even if for the better, will cause some individuals, rather than others, to come into the world. Thus, if we consider the first one hundred years following the introduction of the urban transport law in cities, the people who are born will be completely different to those who would have been born if that law had never been introduced. Hence, and this is Parfit's argument, can we really be sure that the main objective pursued by the people and institutions who adopted those laws will be achieved? Was it not to protect future generations? But who, precisely, has been protected if those measures, or the adoption of a certain law, result in certain people being born rather than others? Altruism in relation to the environment, therefore, is likely to harm the very people it is meant to benefit.

Parfit's position raises two important points. First, our intentions, no matter how noble, can produce unexpected outcomes by generating critical side effects. Second, what lies at the heart of the matter is not future generations, but future individuals. This last point is one stressed by Anthony D'Amato in his treatment of Parfit's paradox, when he underscores how curious it is to think that we can be bound by any sort of obligation towards people who may never exist or who, even if they do come to exist, may be different to how they would have been under different circumstances.[29] D'Amato clearly takes a deflationary approach to the concept of future generations by reducing them to their components, that is, to future individuals.[30] In other words, when we assume we have an obligation towards future generations, what we are really saying is that we have an obligation towards the single individuals who will make up those generations, given that a generation is nothing more than the sum of the individuals that belong to that generation. I will return to this point, as it is quite a sensitive issue, which can perhaps be seen in a different light from a metaphysical perspective. For Parfit and D'Amato's conclusion is not at all neutral from a metaphysical point of view, as it implies, for example, that only individuals exist and that the obligations we undertake towards the future are towards particular entities, such as individuals, and not towards general, abstract or, in a certain sense, vague entities, as generations would appear to be at first sight. Or, as Lothar Gündling emphasizes, it implies that actions aimed at shaping the life of future generations end up, rather undesirably, affecting the identities of the individuals that will make up those generations.[31] It is worth pointing out that the idea of connecting actions aimed at protecting future generations to the protection of their identity is not at all very plausible. There are, indeed, countless cultural, social and historical factors that condition what we are and can be, what we become and can become. Unconditioned identity, in the sense discussed by Gündling, is simply an abstract concept.

On the other hand, the general questions posed by Parfit and D'Amato deserve greater attention, as they lie at the heart of this work. Any policy promoted with a view to protecting transgenerationality – as in this example of environmental policy – will be shaped by at least three factors. The first factor is 'what' we intend to protect, something which we clearly consider to be a good for us and for those who will come after us. The second factor is the 'entity' on whose behalf we decide to pursue protection measures. Parfit and D'Amato suggest that the concept of generations should be reduced to the concept of individuals, meaning that when we talk about 'future generations', what we really want to do is talk about future individuals. If we accept that point and reduce a generation to individuals, then we also have to accept the idea that protecting present individuals, those who live here and now, is something different to protecting future generations. Seeking to protect the future in any way is ultimately a more complex task – full of unknowns – that cannot be left solely to our good faith, as intentions, actions and laws can conceal any number of unforeseeable implications. The weak point theoretically in Parfit's argument is, therefore, the reduction of a generation to individuals, as it is not at all obvious, but rather problematic. It is a matter we will return to in addressing the question of the identity of generations.

The third and final factor concerns 'actions'. The underlying argument is that the transgenerational bond emerges through 'actions'. In the case of secondary transgenerationality, it typically emerges in a specific kind of social action: transgenerational social action. Thus, the structure of such actions needs to be analyzed. To begin with, transgenerational social actions are structurally neutral, in the sense that they are neither positive nor negative. In other words, they neither promote nor detract from the transgenerational bond. The positivity or negativity of transgenerational actions depends on the content of the action. In many cases, people and institutions carry out transgenerational actions without any awareness of the transgenerational structure of the actions. That poses a serious problem not only in terms of the performance of the actions – that is, the ways in which the action can be performed – but above all in terms of their long-term implications. These are more questions we will return to. Once the peculiar structure of transgenerational actions, entailing the necessity of intergenerational cooperation for their effective performance, is acknowledged, social agents who initiate transgenerational actions can no longer evade responsibility for the consequences that may come from those actions. In other words, they must necessarily address the problem of the consequences for future generations.

Finally, the third example concerns the world of work. Work is a sensitive topic for a number of reasons. Work is a fundamental practice in our life, giving rise to assumptions, expectations and the possibility of reward and social advancement. Work is fundamental not just as a means of survival but also in the formation of personal identity.[32] That is true, at least, for Western societies, where personal growth is generally seen to come through achievement in the sphere of work, replacing *otium* with *negotium*, in contrast with the classical tradition. Precisely because of its central importance, work has undergone numerous and profound transformations.[33] It can be observed, for instance, how each industrial revolution (we are now in the fourth, known as Industry 4.0, driven by ICT and other new technologies) has brought about major changes not only in the market but also in the very concept of work itself. All this makes the world of work a particularly significant field of observation for understanding transgenerationality.

Conflict has often swept the world of work. In the nineteenth century and the first half of the twentieth century, it exploded in the form of class conflict. With globalization, conflict has shifted onto the shoulders of individuals, who often live and work in isolation, in unstable and fragmented jobs. Then, at the macroeconomic level, there is conflict between societies that strive to protect workers and the dignity of their pay, and societies that pursue growth and development through widespread deregulation, creating working conditions that undermine the sphere of personal rights. As has been rightly observed,[34] one of the main features of the contemporary world of work is the continuous mobilization of workers. As unemployment levels remain persistently high, people in jobs often find themselves working incredibly long hours each day, even outside traditional workplaces and contexts. It is the typical case of a freedom, that of being able to work in different places, leading to practices that are invasive, to say the least – since we can work anywhere, anytime, we end up doing so, in response to a sort of psychological and material obligation.

The pervasiveness of work plays an important role in determining personal identity, which risks, however, being absorbed by working identity. Paradoxically, we tend to work more even though the development and spread of technology should enable us to work less, and better. Nevertheless, that is not the only problem. There is also another delicate question that has to do, even in this case, with the problems tied to public debt. It is characteristically indicative of the poor health of many Western economies that a large part of revenues from income tax goes to paying the debt contracted by national states. The situation, which is generally not presented with due clarity by governments, is foreseeably destined to fuel social conflict, aggravating generational tensions.

Let us stop and recap. Work is fundamental for people in building their lives, guaranteeing subsistence and a place in society, while constituting a part of personal and social identity. Moreover, the world of work is one of the typical arenas of intergenerational cooperation, a place where transgenerational cooperation may be present and productive, or instead absent, sometimes dramatically so. Here, transgenerationality is affected by the problem of the exploitation and management of the resources available to a community, by the issue of the transfer of the skills present within a labour market and, finally, by the accumulation of wealth or, alternatively, debt that a certain community produces or manages. Let us think, for example, of the problems tied to the progressive ageing of our societies. Statistics show that over the last fifteen years, the age curve of workers, in Europe at least, has risen dramatically. In this regard, labour market analysts generally focus on three issues: the capacity for people to work until old age; the skills needed to ensure quality jobs for the aged through lifelong learning; and finally, generational mobility.[35] As the average life expectancy grows, workers obviously need to work longer to raise the pension needed to support themselves in their lengthening retirement years.

All this entails a number of implications. The first, to begin with, concerns training. Older workers generally have better experience but a lower propensity for reskilling. In a highly competitive and fast changing labour market like our own, training is a strategic lever for the system to remain competitive, especially when considering the fact that machines are gradually replacing humans when it comes to heavier and less creative jobs. That should be good news, given that it suggests how heavy labour and depersonalized jobs are progressively being transferred to machines, continuing a process begun in the first industrial revolution.[36] The not so good news is that the process is neither banal nor automatic, given that to minimize the major collateral damage of that transfer, it calls for human workers who have the opportunity, willingness and capacity for lifelong learning, and hence for the ongoing and substantial overhaul of their skills and professional abilities. That all requires humans to be open to knowledge and intellectual exploration, capable of adapting to a system in constant and extremely rapid transformation (and therefore capable of effectively overcoming both fear and anxiety) and to see self-realization through work as one of their primary goals. On the other hand, if older workers have the right, and the duty, to keep working and to remain productive for longer, new generations have an equal right to a place in the production cycle. Thus, it is the task of the system, and the institutions that govern it, to ensure its permeability by promoting the generational changeover needed, including the effective transfer of skills.

Transgenerationality is best expressed in cooperative and culturally sophisticated contexts. Yet, the human nature from which it ultimately emerges is instinctively and essentially conservative and competitive. Nevertheless, as we will shortly see, an equally decisive human trait is the appreciation of the Other in ever-more sophisticated forms, which is what opens up the possibility of appreciating the value and function of transgenerationality, as well as the importance and meaning of transgenerational actions. Hence it is no coincidence that modern political philosophy should have insisted so much on fear and anxiety being the primary emotions that, perhaps more than any other, shape social behaviour. Fear expresses our sense of precariousness; anxiety anticipates danger. Work lived and experienced as conflict between classes falls within those social arrangements typically aimed at defending a medium-sized group from external threats. If that group is then subject to progressive ageing, the tendency of the group to defend itself will grow, transforming itself into an unassailable phalanx. That, at least, is what will happen unless measures are introduced to promote its permeability at different levels, in terms of generational changeover, the circulation of knowledge and, finally, the creation of wealth. Transferring knowledge is crucial for the system to survive and function, as knowledge generates development and development generates wealth and investments, which produce more knowledge, triggering a virtuous circle. For that virtuous circle to take off, however, it is the world of work, itself made up of a series of sub-worlds, that needs to ensure the transgenerational transfer of skills, knowledge and resources.

Individualism vs solidarity

That a society, or a political institution, is capable of enduring in time has everything to do with transgenerationality. In its primary form, transgenerationality is a biological instinct that ties together members of the same family. In its secondary form, transgenerationality is made up of those actions that tie a generation to the generations that come after it. In other words, secondary transgenerationality is expressed by the effects of all those actions that will necessarily impact the generations to come. The argument underpinning the discussion here is that to understand the ways in which generations build reciprocal relations with each other, it is fundamental to bear in mind the characteristics of human nature. For it is in human nature that the roots of social and political structures lie – in the way humans are made, in their biological and natural constitution. That means that any inquiry investigating the structures of social reality, be it in ontology or social philosophy, must first of all reckon with philosophical anthropology. In other words, it must expressly outline the underlying idea it has of human nature. Human beings build and establish stable relationships within a framework that is primarily biological in nature – the defence, protection and support of children, on the one hand, and the defence of life and individuality, on the other. Love and fear are ultimately, therefore, the primary emotions we are dealing with, the emotions that originally gave impetus to the organization of the social sphere. On the basis of these emotions, and the behaviours they give rise to, various social and political models have been built, forming nuclei that quite clearly are resistant to transformations precisely because their roots lie in biology.

That observation leads to a second point. Love and fear decisively shape the psychology of humans, but they also determine the set-up of the social and political arrangements that human beings have chosen to construct. Those arrangements afford greater importance to space and to all the means we have of shaping and protecting it. Conversely, the ways in which time impacts a social or political entity appear less decisive in how social structures work. To put it another way, the emotions of love, fear, defence and care find expression and topical representation in physical space. That means drawing borders to defend and territories to protect, marked out against the external space inhabited by the Other, by what is diverse – a construction of national identity, which is political and territorial identity. What would appear most pressing politically, therefore, is the defence, organization and conquest of a certain space, or the management of space in the near future. The reasons for such tendencies are, of course, self-evident. It is not easy dealing with the future, and any attempt to do so will mean bearing the burden of the consequences of our actions and hence radically changing the terms of our relationship with all that surrounds us. Vice versa, the effective management of space permits us at least to protect the objects of our love and to control our fear. Thus, it enables us to manage all that would immediately appear to be most urgent.

That explains, in part at least, why the issue of transgenerationality and the questions connected with it have been so widely neglected in social philosophy, political thought and social ontology. It also explains how such a lengthy and generalized neglect has led to such major damage. The near-total attention focused on controlling space over the short or very near term has driven societies and governments to ignore a fundamental matter of fact, which is that the more complex our societies become, the more bonds we build that endure at length in time. While the endurance of such bonds is a necessary condition for the survival of society, it also exhibits peculiar characteristics, which, as we will see, call for greater attention and study in both ethical and legal terms. And that is because, in general, it gives rise to a phenomenon which is shaping the way Western democracies work, as individuals and institutions show an opportunistic approach when dealing with transgenerationality. That is, when they can benefit from it, they acknowledge it; instead, when they ought to take responsibility for the duties it entails, by thinking of the consequences of their actions, they ignore it.

Complex systems require time for their potential to unfold completely and for decisions to be implemented fully, and hence for complex actions to be accomplished. Thus, the temporal continuity necessary for their accomplishment can only be guaranteed by cooperation across different generations. A life form, such as the human being, that only thinks in terms of the battle for survival will tend to assume the necessity of biological fact (the instinct for self-preservation) and organize its social and political structures accordingly. The outcome will be social systems that are highly competitive and focused on issues connected with the defence and protection of individuals and social and political institutions. That, in effect, is what political philosophy has theorized ever since Hobbes. Such a state of affairs entails a deficiency of solidarity – in particular, as we will see, a deficiency of transgenerational solidarity, which is especially significant in complex societies.

Many good reasons exist to work on the construction of a society based on solidary models, and hence models promoting transgenerational solidarity rather than focusing on individualism. Over the course of this book, that point will be explored in relation to the idea of a social and political model which is sensitive to transgenerational issues. The argument will attempt to prove that societies which privilege an individualist model suffer a deficiency of transgenerational solidarity. But what is it and how can we recognize it? To answer that question, first the concept of solidarity needs to be analyzed.[37] To begin with, it should be noted that the term, in its most widespread meaning, encompasses both descriptive and normative elements. We can shed light on that ambiguity by looking at the Roman legal institution of *obligatio in solidum*, which was transposed into the Napoleonic Code of 1804 as the joint and several interest of debtors,[38] where they are 'all obliged for one and the same thing, such that each is liable for the entirety'.[39] Scholz[40] sets out an initial taxonomy of forms of social solidarity, identifying at one extreme family members and at the other individuals who share a certain objective. The criteria used to shape that taxonomy are the interdependency of the members of a certain group and the degree to which objectives and common interests are shared. Objectives and common interests, however, are not a sufficient condition for the adoption of solidary behaviour, as such factors could, for example, give rise to forms of competition that can be quite aggressive. Individuals, for instance, could choose to compete rather than collaborate without considering, or by not considering sufficiently positive, the benefits that would come from the adoption of solidary behaviour.

It should additionally be stressed how solidarity does not appear to imply any reference to moral standards, given that in some crime syndicates, and certainly in Mafia organizations, the members of the group are solidary in their behaviour, without however, showing any morality of a universal nature in their actions.[41] A long list of films that capture the essence – epic in its own way – of Mafia organizations, such as *The Godfather* or *Once Upon a Time in America*, narrate that apparent contradiction quite well, where the members of the Mafia clan commit any number of absolutely immoral actions but are completely solidary among themselves. To the point that solidarity is necessary and essential for the life of the group.

Thus, for solidarity to emerge in a certain context, at least two conditions are necessary: (1) the cohesion of the group; and (2) cooperation aimed at the production of a common good.[42] Furthermore, another recurring element that would often appear to be found is some sort of affective involvement, at least in cases involving solidarity among people. Given, therefore, that solidarity is a relationship that emerges from the relationship between different agents (people, groups of people, and institutions, at the least), we can adopt the distinction made by Raimo Tuomela, who identifies three types of solidarity: (a) internal group solidarity, where a social bond implies coordination and cooperation between the members of a group. The idea is that if a group is capable of collective action, then it shows a certain degree of internal group solidarity; (b) external group solidarity, where the cooperative and coordinated action of an internally solidary group is aimed at satisfying the requests of a group-external party, which may be an individual or a collective group; and finally, (c) humanitarian or moral solidarity, where a moral obligation is recognized towards other agents as members of humankind, grounded on a universalizing ethics.[43] Therefore, solidarity appears to imply the existence of a group of people who feel they are united or feel some form of connection and who share a common vision or, in more practical terms, common objectives. Within that framework, mutual support can be manifested through targeted action.

The idea that solidarity arises between people who share something follows from the assumption that the existence of solidarity implies the existence of common properties shared by the individuals who make up a certain group. Furthermore, in the second type of solidarity identified by Tuomela, solidarity can be extended to people who do not belong to the group, but who share and support the reasons for which the group exists. That form of solidarity requires concrete and differentiated ties – namely, the concrete relationship that enables solidary bonds to be formed. But not all forms of solidarity, however, are built on concrete ties. This last idea is captured by Tuomela in his third type of solidarity, which shows a certain affinity with David Wiggins's conception of moral solidarity as a primitive form of recognition between human beings: 'If I can recognize the other, then he or she can recognize me in the same way.'[44] The idea here is that the absence of personal ties is not a hindrance, at least not in all situations. It is no coincidence that Wiggins develops his argument in relation to Hume,[45] who circumscribed the sociopolitical dimension to the sphere of family and friends. In other words, for Hume, human beings are social and political animals only to the extent that they are tied by the sentiments of love and friendship. When that is not the case, what ties them is merely a stipulation, an agreement that typically serves to achieve an objective.[46] That is precisely the argument challenged by Wiggins, namely, the idea that solidary behaviour only takes place in circumscribed contexts. Instead, he argues that it is always possible to identify a core that enables us to recognize humans and respond to humans in solidary ways. Quoting Simone Weil,[47] he talks of a right to recognition of every person simply as a person, which every human being expects from other human beings. It is a demand (and a need) that is evident in particularly dramatic situations – situations in which all the details that make up a life withdraw into the background and all that remains in the foreground becomes what is characteristically human, pure and simple.

Now, the three possible types of solidarity identified by Tuomela are obviously not all on the same level. What distinguishes them is how concrete the reference is. It is not easy to feel solidarity for humankind because such a form of solidarity exists on the abstract and logical plane, whereas solidarity, and more generally the sentiments we feel, towards a circumscribed and identifiable group of people has the advantage of being concrete in its reference and in the type of relationship that binds each to the other. From what we have said so far, it follows that the solidary bond originates in primary transgenerationality, or the bond between members of the same family or between friends. Instead, things are different when it comes to secondary transgenerationality, or the bond that emerges and binds people who have no direct ties. Thus, if we want societies and states to endure in time and to promote fairness, it is necessary to introduce a form of transgenerational solidarity, or solidarity between generations, to replace individualism. For that to be possible, the normative plane obviously cannot be neglected, in the sense that, where people do not spontaneously grasp the benefits of taking a transgenerational perspective, institutions should do so instead, supporting it through law.

But let us put first things first and turn now to the origins of primary transgenerationality. Nature and human beings.

2

Anthropology

Transgenerationality and Recognition

What the human being is not: An ontology of the human

To outline the philosophical anthropology that underpins the idea of transgenerationality I wish to propose, I will first attempt to deconstruct two theories that, in different ways and in different times, underlie modern and contemporary political philosophy. They are the regulatory idea for which human beings can behave in perfectly rational ways, and the theory that the political dimension is dominated by the emotion of fear[1] and by the form of the individual. After deconstructing those two theories, I will move on to describe a relational anthropological model based on the notion of recognition put forward by Hegel in his Jena writings, which was applied by Georg Herbert Mead in psychology. I believe the notion of recognition lends itself particularly well to framing the question of transgenerational bonds appropriately.[2]

Let us begin, therefore, with the deconstruction of the first theory, which holds that human beings behave, or can behave, or again, should behave as perfectly rational agents. As much as we might debate whether humans one day will indeed be so inclined, today we know for sure that humans are not rational in any number of circumstances in which they are called to make a decision. Countless examples demonstrate this.[3] First, however, I will start with a preliminary consideration. All political philosophies are based and shaped by underlying anthropological assumptions. If those assumptions are flawed or, worse, wrong, the political philosophy derived from them will similarly be flawed or wrong. A good example is a short book considered a touchstone for anarchic theories entitled *In Defense of Anarchism*, written by the American philosopher Robert Wolff.

As is widely known, the book looks at the contradictions inherent in the concept of the state, given the conflict between political authority and moral autonomy. Wolff argues that the authority of the state, by its nature, or by nature of the demands it makes of its citizens, is incompatible with the autonomy of which individuals cannot be deprived in the moral sphere. In other words, if we assume that personal responsibility cannot be forfeited, we cannot at the same time conclude that individuals should delegate a part of their rights and duties to the state. To do so would mean alienating a part of their autonomy and restricting their own freedom. Now, the purpose here is not so much to discuss the central idea of the book as to put forward a few observations on the anthropological assumptions supporting Wolff's theory in the third and final chapter. In particular, he significantly assumes that the state is the construct of a stipulation made by the contracting parties to its foundational pact, and as such it is an institution that can be dismantled the moment in which the individuals who founded it, or their descendants, no longer have any need for it and can therefore live without it. And that will happen once completely rational humans, in full knowledge of the immediate and long-term consequences of their actions, decide to rein in their private interests to pursue the common good, or in Wolff's words:

> The state is a social institution, and therefore no more than the totality of the beliefs, expectations, habits, and interacting roles of its members and subjects. When rational men, in full knowledge of the proximate and distant consequences of their actions, determine to set private interest aside and pursue the general good, it *must* be possible for them to create a form of association which accomplishes that end without depriving some of them of their moral autonomy. The state, in contrast to nature, cannot be ineradicably *other*.[4]

Therefore, since the state is a social construction, if that condition of human development were to be reached, it can be concluded that it would be possible to live in total freedom, outside the organization of a state:

> Our failure to discover a form of political association which could combine moral autonomy with legitimate authority is not a result of the imperfect

rationality of men, nor of the passions and private interests which deflect men from the pursuit of justice and the moral good. Many political philosophers have portrayed the state as a necessary evil forced upon men by their own inability to abide by the principles of morality, or as a tool of one class of men against the others in the never-ending struggle for personal advantage. Marx and Hobbes agree that in a community of men of good will, where the general good guided every citizen, the state would be unnecessary.[5]

Essentially, Wolff supposes that with good will, firm intelligence and full knowledge humans would be able to live outside rigid normative arrangements such as those of a state. And they would be able to enjoy total freedom to decide, as they would be completely responsible for their actions. Now, to understand to what extent Wolff's ideas can be considered realistic, I believe it can help to reflect on what I shall call human ontology, which lies at the foundation of philosophical anthropology and the development of political thought. That will lead to the deconstruction of one of the cardinal ideas of modern political philosophy, which is the centrality of fear in defining humans.

The first observation to make is rather self-evident, but nonetheless important. Humans are not abstract objects, they are entirely concrete in the fundamental traits of their nature. Any good human ontology will therefore take such an awareness as its starting point. Modern political thought never fails to describe human nature to us, focusing on the traits that resist any sort of cultural change. Niccolò Machiavelli, for instance, sums them up as follows:

> For of men it may generally be affirmed that they are thankless, fickle, false studious to avoid danger, greedy of gain, devoted to you while you are able to confer benefits upon them, and ready, as I said before, while danger is distant, to shed their blood, and sacrifice their property, their lives, and their children for you; but in the hour of need they turn against you.[6]

In a certain way, a continuous thread joins Machiavelli and Wolff. The former relates the unreliable and aggressive nature of human beings (something that is assumed by all individualistic political philosophies); the latter, without denying that point, adds that if humans were to learn to behave in completely rational ways, they would be able to do away with institutions like the state that serve, in large part, to protect them from their own individualism.

Individualistic theories assume that human beings are competitive and aggressive monads, exposed to fear and saved, at times, by courage.

Thoughts on the progress of human civilization

One of the issues most widely explored in political and social philosophy is that of the progress, or civilization, of humankind. The general idea is that humans began to give rise to increasingly complex social and political institutions to escape the 'state of nature' – a dimension that lies between the real and fantastical, which is believed to have characterized the pre-social stage of human development. The state of nature, or the somewhat extravagant picture that philosophy has at times depicted of that peculiar moment in human history, is thought to have had rather precise characteristics. To begin with, what we can suppose of that time has its origins in two 'conceits', as Vico calls them: the conceit of nations and the conceit of scholars. Both would appear to have sought to ennoble the origins of human history. Vico attributes the shaping of that great mire, which is the origin of history, to poets, whose metaphysics he claims has its origins in poetic knowledge. Two branches spread from the trunk of that metaphysics: on the one hand, logic, morality, economics and politics; on the other, physics, the mother of cosmography and astronomy.

> And we will make it possible to see, in each of these clear and distinct fashions, how the founders of gentile humanity by their natural theology – that is, their metaphysics – imagined the gods; how by their logic they discovered languages; how by their morality they generated the heroes; how by their economics they founded families, by their politics, cities. We will show how by their physics, they established principles of all the divine things; how by a physics particular to man, they, in a certain mode, generated their very selves; how by their cosmography, they devised an entire universe of gods; how by their astronomy they brought the planets and the constellations from Earth to the heavens; how by their chronology they offered a beginning to historical times; and by their geography, the Greeks, for the sake of example, described the world within Greece itself.[7]

Vico imagines that at the dawn of history the world was populated by giants, huge brutes whose identity was distinctively marked by their physical strength and relationship with nature. In that first stage, humanity was divided between those of regular height (the Hebrew people) and the giants. He held that it was fear, together with more attentive bodily cleansing practices, that brought the giants down to the right size, namely, the height of humans. Superincumbent nature – Vico speaks of bolts of lightning striking with great violence – then compelled the giants to raise their eyes to the heavens and seek the causes of the phenomena hanging over them. It was precisely the brutes, therefore, who initiated that incredibly powerful imaginative process that would lead to the birth of the nations – a process all the more profound and powerful because it depended on the likes of those whose nature was so closely bound up with their corporeality. Their imagination depended necessarily on their corporeality and retained all its ties to the senses and the passions. Those ties were the same that bound the first poets to the matter of their poetic imagination. It was those giants, endowed with a poetic imagination so powerfully tied to their corporeality and passions, who raised their eyes and saw the heavens. They were the ones who would give shape to the first divinities and to the world with an imaginative force that we can only just barely conceive.

Vico stresses the hypothetical and symbolic nature of his reconstruction of the dawn of world history. Nevertheless, putting aside the metaphors, it would appear to make some sense to posit the evolution of the human animal as moving from the sensible dimension (and hence disproportionately made up of emotions and passions) to the rational dimension:

> So, in our time, it is naturally denied to us to enter into the vast imaginary of those earliest men, whose minds had nothing abstract, subtle, or spiritualized about them, for they were completely immersed in the senses, completely buffeted by the passions, completely buried in the body. Hence, as we said above, in our time, it is nearly impossible to understand and completely impossible to imagine how they would have thought, these earliest men who founded gentile humanity.[8]

Anticipating the observations of Friedrich Nietzsche in *On Truth and Lies in a Nonmoral Sense*, Vico notes how the giants ended up believing in what they themselves had created, namely, in the gods with which they themselves had populated their world, and in the division between good and evil that they themselves had created by inventing morality. Vico discerns how that very early part of human history unfolded through the mediation of corporeality – 'the contemplation of the heavens done with the eyes of the body'[9] – and how such an exuberance of corporeality must have been tamed by the authority of the gods, to begin with, and then of humans. That authority marked the start of the exercise of the will, which established its dominion over the movement of those oversized bodies. Thanks to the exercise of control and peace, the gradual passage towards a more civil form of life was made possible.

Before moving on, it is worth stopping to note some important points. First of all, the fact that Vico considers human history to be guided by a developmental process that is shaped, so to speak, by a sensibility for the logos. Secondly, the fact that he universalizes that process, treating it as a necessary step for the development of all nations. Then there is poetic language, which Vico sees as the fundamental language enabling such development to unfold. Finally, there is the assumption that since the civil world, or social reality, as we would say, was made by humans, humans can, and so ought to, identify its principles. Thus, there is development in history and of history, a development that is measured by the evolution of human nature. Indeed, the underlying idea, which Vico shares with Hobbes, sees anthropocentrism, a constituent tendency in human reasoning, as one of the dispositions that leads to radical errors. If, as would appear evident, a clear anthropocentrism guides humans in formulating judgements and in imaginatively reconstructing those parts of historical reality that, for a diversity of reasons, remain obscure or unknown to us, then it is easy to understand the reasons why nations and scholars, in reasoning about the development of human affairs, have done so by transferring into their conception of the remotest antiquity models that are totally absurd, and hence false. That is the conceit of nations and the conceit of scholars, which seeks to read in universal terms what is ultimately none other than an anthropological construction.

In contrast to Hobbes, therefore, Vico believes that the origins of humankind should be sought in a form of life displaying characteristics in part different from our own, in the overabundance of sensibility and emotion that was reined back into just measure only thanks to the adoption of religion. The point of divergence with Hobbes,[10] apart from the metaphor adopted, revolves around whether the dawn of human history was populated by humans with the same characteristics as the moderns.[11] For Vico, human nature has witnessed a certain evolution. The mastery of the rational dimension and of the measure of the passions required a certain process and a capacity to impose measure, equilibrium and order. Thus, the main driver of human history lies in poetic creation, that is, in the imagination and fantasy, whereas philosophy, or rational thought, comes later, following at a certain distance. Such evolution comes through precise stages: 'The order of human things proceeds so that, first, there are forests; later, lodges; thereafter, villages; then, cities; and finally, academies.'[12] With regard to human nature, Vico speaks clearly:

> Consequently, we establish that man in the bestial state loves only his own safety; when he takes on a spouse and has children, he loves his own safety along with the safety of families; when he arrives at civil life, he loves his own safety along with the safety of the city; when he extends power over people other than his own, he loves his own safety along with the safety of those nations; and when nations unite in wars, peace, alliances, or commerce, he loves his own safety along with the safety of the whole of humankind. In all these circumstances, man principally loves his own advantage.[13]

Hence, the underlying idea is that, when we consider human nature, we must certainly bear in mind how it has known a certain evolution that goes from an original semi-animal dimension – the age of the giants – to the strictly human dimension. In short, that same humankind that builds social and institutional structures of ever-growing complexity bears within it an animal core, albeit one that is greatly weakened. Therefore, even after having long abandoned the way of life of the giants, human beings continue to be interested first of all in *their own safety* and second in the safety of the people and institutions closest to them. The notion is that, however much their sphere of interest is broadened, humans remain concerned first and foremost with their survival and their gain. Although he historicizes the matter of origin, and by doing so distinguishes himself from Hobbes, Vico still holds to the idea that sociality develops from an essentially individualistic basis, and that fear is the dominant social emotion. Thus, Vico's alternative to the social contract nevertheless draws from a human ontology that in many ways is akin to that described by Hobbes.

Homo homini lupus

'To speak impartially, both sayings are very true; That Man to Man is a kind of God; and that Man to Man is an errant Wolfe. The first is true, if we compare

Citizens amongst themselves; and the second, if we compare Cities.'[14] As the 1600s wore on, bringing political turbulence and strife, Hobbes decided to turn his efforts to understanding why humans showed such a passion for wars. One reason probably lay in their nature, in the very way humans are made. For human nature is such that humans fear the strength of their peers, the only thing that really can hold them back. That means humans have a tendency, by natural disposition, not for harmony, but for conflict, whether to preserve themselves or to overpower others.

Hobbes is very precise in drawing an important distinction. If, on the one hand, humans seem naturally to be sociable animals (children need to be nurtured until an advanced age and adults, to live well, need to belong to a social context), on the other, such a trait would appear to emerge only in rather restricted contexts. That is to say, the disposition to rear offspring and to care for others rarely applies outside the spheres of family and friendship. Thus, Hobbes concludes that humans may well be a social animal, but the reach of their rationality is rather limited by nature. What instead appears to be universal for Hobbes is the human disposition outside the sphere of civil society. That pre-civil state, which Vico describes as a state in evolution, is for Hobbes a state that he identifies as having determinate, clearly recognizable characteristics. And what characterizes the state of nature above all, distinguishing it from civil society, is the disposition for the war of all against all.[15] For in the state of nature, every man has the right to everything, and consequently, he has the right to make use of every means to obtain what he has a right to.

State of nature

The concept of the state of nature, as described by Hobbes, stands at the antithesis of Vico's historical approach. It cannot be understood without reference to the philosophical anthropology on which it is based, which means it cannot be understood without first putting into focus all the elements that make up the broader sphere of humankind. Hobbes derives those elements directly from the animal nature of humans, that is, by identifying animality as the empirical basis of humanity. The Aristotelian and Scholastic tradition of political thought instead held that man is by nature a political animal, in the sense that humans are naturally disposed to sociality and sympathy. From that assumption it was then derived that society has natural foundations too, as it is founded on the natural disposition of individuals for sociality.

Hobbes's conception of the state of nature dismantles that argument from its very foundations. For Hobbes, what drove, and still drives, humans to live in society was nothing to do with their supposedly natural tendency to be social, but rather the search for some sort of gain generally to be had from social life. The truth of this can easily be seen, argues Hobbes, by observing how humans diversify the social relationships they hold. It is evident how people generally comport themselves differently with others depending on the circumstances and on the benefits that can be derived. Thus, societies are built on the gains that human beings can, or believe they can, draw from them. The gains that Hobbes has in mind are directly tied to the sphere of survival and the characteristics of the state of nature. So let us start from there, specifically, the imaginary conditions lying at the origins of human history, which Hobbes describes as the conditions characterizing the state of pre-social humans.

The peculiarity of the state of nature lies in its perfect equality, while the sentiment characterizing it is fear, as Vico would later theorize. The situation of perfect equality, as described by Hobbes, is as singular as it is artificial, as all human beings in the state of nature are perfectly equal from all points of view, by virtue of which they can aspire to obtain anything and everything they believe they necessitate. Little does it matter if nature has endowed some with greater or lesser physical strength, others with greater or lesser intelligence and yet others with courage. What ultimately counts is the legitimacy and indeterminacy of their desire, which virtually leads them to want everything. It is obviously implausible to think that humans by nature are born equal from all points of view, such as, and above all, in terms of their physical strength and cognitive ability. Hobbes defends his argument against the contrary argument put forth by Aristotle in the *Politics*.[16] Aristotle asserts that some men are born with a disposition to command, others with a disposition to serve, and as such they are, and should be, considered unequal by nature. Hobbes responds by bringing together two levels of argument: the level of experience and the level of pure theory. Now, while the observation of experience clearly offers little in the way of support for equality, it must be said that Hobbes's argument on the theoretical plane has a lot going for it: 'Whether therefore men be equal by nature, the equality is to be acknowledged; or whether unequal, because they are like to contest for dominion, it is necessary for the obtaining of peace, that they be esteemed as equal.'[17]

That desire knows no limits – which is legitimate in this case, given that the state of nature is founded on unlimited desire, or a desire in any case commensurate with the needs of the person – arguably represents the main cause of instability, as would be discovered centuries later by psychoanalysis. Hobbes considers desire to be one of the main causes of war. And war, as we know, can lead to virtually devastating social disgregation. Thus, a limit must be placed on one of the most concrete causes of death. In that sense, overcoming the state of nature and attempting to place a limit on unlimited desire are, for Hobbes, one and the same thing, as the passage from the state of nature to a civil state also marks the passage from the unlimited to the limited, or the containment of desire.

The crux of the matter is, therefore, clearly tied to the question of utility. Equality reigns in the state of nature, but equality is evidently not the key to a good life, if anything it threatens a perpetual state of war. Alongside the question of utility, there is another fundamental matter, which is that of power, often tied to the dynamics of recognition. Essentially, it is not only for material gain that men and women go against their natural dispositions to join in association. They also do so because such associations enable the dimension of perpetual war to be managed more advantageously, while permitting the construction of power structures in the social sphere. Such structures make it possible to express strength and superiority in highly sublimated ways – something to which Nietzsche would return two centuries after Hobbes with great incisiveness.

In the state of nature, therefore, humans contend to obtain what is good for them and flee from what they hold to be bad. Thus, it is a right of nature for humans to make use of all means at their disposal to protect their lives and their bodies, as far as within their power. Now for fear. Hobbes is careful to make the distinction between fear and dread, stressing how the emotion distinguishing the state of nature (a return to which is always possible under determinate conditions) is fear,[18] not dread. Therefore, the primary emotion that drives humans to join together is not sympathy, or the sentiment of feeling bound to a collective, and in some way empathetic dimension, but rather fear.[19] For Hobbes, fear is the other face of the total freedom (of intent and means) enjoyed by humans in the state of nature. In a world in which every desire is legitimate, as is every means pursued to satisfy it, the sense of insecurity and alert – fear – proves to be the predominant emotional force.

It is in this framework of maximum freedom coupled with maximum insecurity that reason steps in, through the formulation of the laws of nature. The first law of nature is the law suggesting that the rights tied to the state of nature – the right to desire everything and hence the right to have everything – ought to be abandoned. The turning point, or rather the means, that Hobbes identifies for changing the rules of the game is the covenant, which consists in the conveyance of a right. To secure greater protection, therefore, the inhabitants of the state of nature are called to give up certain fundamental rights, thereby placing precise limits on their freedom.

The situation Hobbes imagines is highly unrealistic in a number of ways, first of all in its idea that nothing in the state of nature is capable of overturning the absolute equality he presumes. Such an idea in itself appears rather bizarre, given that in conditions such as those believed to hold in early human history, dissimilarities in physical strength would surely have made a significant difference, as Vico sensibly notes. Then there are the means posited by Hobbes to explain the passage from the state of nature to the social state, which are incredibly utopian. Such a step was apparently made possible by the collective and simultaneous transfer, by means of covenant, of the rights of all the human beings living in a certain state of nature to a person (or an assembly) willing to accept them. For that process to come to a satisfactory conclusion, a solid relationship of trust must be established among the members of the one community, and the act of renouncing the rights must be simultaneous. In other words, all the members of the state of nature need to convey the same rights at the same time.

In his thought experiment, Hobbes evidently assumes a very high level of awareness – an awareness that is pre-theoretical – in all the members of the community in the state of nature. The assumption is particularly interesting, and particularly charged with philosophical implications, as the state of nature that the English philosopher imagines ideally comes before the social dimension of political life. Thus, where Vico, roughly speaking, posits beasts, Hobbes instead sees human beings capable of sophisticated theoretical abstraction, as the process of transferring rights required to mark the passage to civil society implies full awareness of the costs (the rights each individual gives up) and benefits (the greater safety and security attained) involved. Hence, putting aside the matter of philosophical modelling, Hobbes's conception really does seem implausible. So let us now turn to how the advent of civil society more plausibly came about by exploring whether the idea of an unconscious practice coming to consciousness over history, as suggested by both Vico and Hegel, is any better in capturing the emergence of the social dimension.

Covenants and contracts

Hobbes provides a very precise description of the terms and methods for the conveyance of rights. To begin with, both those who convey rights and those who receive them must consent to the transfer. It follows that rights cannot be conveyed unwittingly or by the dictates of custom. Thus, our earlier supposition, that Hobbes's intuition should be considered a well-constructed thought experiment which, nevertheless, has little or nothing to do with the realities of history, would appear to be true. In Hobbes's framework, rights can only be conveyed through methods that are intelligible, using words relating only to the present or the past. It can make no sense to say something along the lines of 'I will promise to pay back the money.' Covenants and promises imply a commitment of the will, so it makes no sense to say today that I shall commit my will tomorrow. I can only state my intention to commit my will now, as I write, or confirm that I already committed it yesterday, but in any case I cannot promise to do so in the future. On this point, Hobbes speaks clearly[20]: 'But if I shall speak of the *time present*, suppose thus; *I doe give* or *have given* you this to be received to morrow, by these words is signified that I have *already given it*, and that his *Right* to receive it *to morrow*, is conveyed to him by me *to day*.'[21]

Such a specification is interesting in its implications, for it means that words alone do not suffice, when relating to the future, to guarantee the meaning and the extent of a commitment of the will. Commitments can only be given in the present or described as having been given in the past. And that is true, first of all, because any declaration of will is founded on a relationship of trust between the person giving the commitment and the person who chooses to rely on the commitment:

but no signe can be given, that he, who us'd future words toward him who was in no sort engag'd to return a benefit, should desire to have his words so understood, as to oblige himselfe thereby. Nor is it suitable to Reason, that those who are easily enclined to doe well to others, should be oblig'd by every promise, testifying their present good affection.[22]

In other words, you can always change your mind until the commitment given, formulated by covenant, becomes a declaration of will. From that moment on, the covenant cannot be redetermined with any ease. Hobbes reinforces several aspects of his theory that imply the revocation of the political covenant, although such a prospect strikes him as most inauspicious.

The model Hobbes has in mind is of a unilateral transfer of a right to a third party, to someone who is under no obligation to return the benefit received, but simply accepts it. It is clear how the English philosopher seeks to preserve the autonomy of the will as far as possible, in terms of the right to revoke until the very last the imperativeness of any commitment. That means we can declare our will here and now, or confirm having declared it in the past, but we cannot assert with any certainty that we will do so in the future, for which any such assertion cannot constitute an obligation to keep the promise.

Therefore, as Hobbes explains, a covenant is valid and binding from the moment we make it, until as long as is necessary to fulfil it. The mutual conveyance of rights between two or more persons is defined as a contract. Where rights are conveyed instantly by all the parties involved, the contract is thereby ended. On the other hand, we can imagine cases in which a contract is based on a declaration of future will, where one or all the contracting parties promise to perform their respective part in the future, in exchange for something already received. In that case, we have a covenant. A covenant made in that way is binding on the will of the contracting parties, obliging them to perform their promises.

The performance of covenants or, if we prefer, the performance of the declarations of will that lead the parties to make the covenants, is a matter of central importance for Hobbes. It is imperative that covenants be performed, as they hold up the social system. Essentially speaking, covenants determine that certain things happen in the world through precise dynamics, first of all because they are underpinned by a system of more or less coercive rules, and then because they are propped up by a general system in which social agents on the whole show mutual trust in each other.

The state of nature is only effectively left behind when humans commit to transferring certain rights and then effectively transfer them. If that does not happen, because people do not keep their promises, the passage to civil society is destined to fail. Nevertheless, the mechanism is extremely delicate, as its effective ability to function is directly tied to at least two factors being in equilibrium, where the first is the degree to which fear drives humans to abandon the state of war of all against all, while the second is their trust in the performance of a covenant entailing the relinquishment of the right to all. How compatible those two factors are with each other is something Hobbes neglects to address, but given the anthropological framework he builds, it is far from self-evident. To put it another way, how is it possible for people who have feared, fought and defied each other to simply start trusting each other at a certain point? That is, not only to start strategically taking into account how a higher good, that of preserving life outside of the state of war, can be pursued but also to actually start trusting both in the fact that other human beings will similarly relinquish their right to 'everything' and in the fact, something by no means obvious, that they will all understand that relinquishment is strategically and politically the most effective means of achieving such an outcome. There is a limit, however, on the validity of covenants. Covenants can only be made in relation to actions that fall under our deliberation. That is, we cannot commit to things or actions that lie completely beyond our control. Thus, covenants and promises only concern the sphere of what is possible and can come to pass.

Hobbes, therefore, divides human history into two stages, one that comes before and another that comes after the civil state. The state of nature thus appears to lie outside the reach of any historical determination. Hobbes's picture of the state of nature turns on the paradox of his idea of virtual equality, where inequalities in physical and cognitive terms play no role whatsoever in the state of nature. A world that is virtually anarchic and depicted in the bleakest of shades, where fear is the only emotional tone and the sole element driving humans to reorganize their way of living. It is only from that exact moment onwards, from when humans decide to limit their freedom, that Hobbes begins to provide a more articulate investigation of the structures and dynamics of civil life.

The picture that emerges from Hobbes's description is altogether rather singular, as a world depicted in black and white suddenly comes to life in colour once humans move from the state of nature into the dimension of the civil state. Something that quite simply, and quite evidently, is just unrealistic. Let us take, for example, the complexity of the emotional and psychological dimension of human beings. First of all, it is not right to reduce the categories of the political to a single emotion, that of fear. In this regard, Hobbes tells one part of the story but loses sight of the greater picture; even the part he tells is far from complete. The phenomenology of the emotions concerning the political or, more broadly, the social sphere are certainly more complex than Hobbes would have us believe. Second, the phenomenology of fear calls for some distinction, as it implies at least two facets, those of defence and offence, which cannot always be distinguished clearly and at times mask each other. Hobbes captures both those aspects and, rather curiously, draws a clear line of separation between them. For him, the predominant emotion in the state of nature is fear, experienced as the need to defend and preserve life. To overcome that sentiment – which is more than a mere sensation, but which derives from a state of affairs where a political dimension in which to frame social life is lacking – the necessity is grasped to relinquish everything by relinquishing the right to obtain everything.

That, however, is only one description of fear. The best form of defence is attack, some would say. Out of fear we can choose to shut ourselves away, defend ourselves or delegate our defence to others; but out of fear we can also choose to attack before being attacked, expanding the sphere of dominion of our being. Fear can lead us to overpower others out of the genuine dread of ending up overpowered. Thus, the phenomenology of Hobbesian emotions is far too limited generally, and more specifically it is lacking in any analysis of the emotion that lies at the foundation of Hobbesian phenomenology: fear. Out of fear we defend ourselves, but out of fear we can also attack.

The zero state of life: Apperception and will

The situation Hobbes imagines is unrealistic not only in the dynamics it outlines but also in the consequences triggered by those dynamics. If the means by which humans move from the state of nature to the civil state are purely hypothetical, giving us the pieces of an elaborate thought experiment, the consequences are no less so, as becomes clear if we take a closer look at Hobbes's idea by which the mechanism defusing fear lies in the relinquishment of 'everything' and the transfer of rights. Ultimately, what Hobbes describes is a rather simple process. In any case, the concept that fear has to do with the instinct for self-preservation deserves a bit more attention than what Hobbes dedicates to it. The instinct for self-preservation has an active component to it, as highlighted by both Arthur Schopenhauer and Nietzsche, which is the other face of fear. Significantly, neither Schopenhauer nor Nietzsche mention fear. Rather, Schopenhauer speaks of the will and Nietzsche of the will to power, suggesting that fear is perhaps the most evident epiphenomenon of a complex entanglement of more primitive primary instincts.

Schopenhauer, in particular, develops his idea of will from what arguably looks a bit like a version 2.0 of the Hobbesian state of nature. In his youth, the philosopher had been initiated by his father into a merchant career, a world in which a certain aggressiveness was the order of the day, though obviously it was not the same struggle for survival posited by Hobbes and Vico. Nevertheless, Schopenhauer's insight opens up a theoretically interesting point about the modern, civilized world, which is that, however much it has lost the crudeness and immediate violence characterizing the struggle for survival in the pre-civil stage, those traits persist nonetheless in a progressively sublimated and partially transformed state. Thus, for all that they may not seem immediately evident to us, those traits still survive in us, and that is why Schopenhauer does not speak of fear, but of 'will'.

The will then leads us to a second element of fundamental importance in anthropological terms, which is that of apperception, or the consciousness a person has of herself and her body. Schopenhauer's idea is that what common sense regards as the subject is the unity of subjective and objective experience, where the subject perceives itself in those two ways. It is, in other words, both the immediate object and agent of self-perception. That immediacy of self-perception, or what is immediately self-evident to the subject, is what we call will. In the ontology Schopenhauer outlines, the body plays a fundamental role because it is what allows the will to express itself extrinsically, to assume visible form and take hold of the world.[23] There is no discontinuity or distinction between will and corporeality. Rather, one is the continuation of the other, as will takes on physical consistency in the body. Schopenhauer speaks plainly in saying that the body is the extrinsic expression of the will:

> The parts of the body must therefore correspond perfectly to the principle desires through which the will manifests itself, these parts must be the visible expression of the desires: teeth, throat and intestines are objectified hunger; the genitals are objectified sex drive; prehensile hands and swift feet correspond to the more indirect strivings of the will they present.[24]

The subject is first of all something that wills because it perceives itself as an entity that wills – and it wills what the body concretely manifests to it, as the body literally takes the form of will. It is interesting to note how Schopenhauer offers a description of the body that anticipates the idea expressed more fully by Nietzsche, whereby the subject is a force that wills itself, and by doing so apperceives itself, that is, it perceives its own unity and identity, and at the same time concretely expresses that identity through what it wills and in what it wills. Which is to say, there is something far more basic than fear, something that makes fear possible, just as it makes other expressions of being possible. That something is the very root of the living being, which is apperception, understood not as a neutral instinct, but as an instinct that is teleologically oriented towards the self-preservation and growth of the being. Or rather, when the will to power is healthy, which in Nietzschean terms means the individual is healthy, will is essentially expressed in terms of growth.

The point is one of the elements that distinguishes Nietzsche from Spinoza, who considered *conatus*,[25] the striving for self-preservation, as the fundamental essence of the living being: 'Every single thing endeavours as far as it lies in itself to persevere in its own being.'[26] Before it fears, the will wills. The relevant point here is the notion of will, which Nietzsche translates in terms of the will to power. The will to power is the will that wills itself, in the sense of willing its own self-preservation and its own growth. That ultimately is what gives rise to fear, or the will's feeling of not having sufficient resources at its disposal to grow its capacity to bear on the world. Nietzsche transforms Schopenhauer's principle into a monist principle through which reality can be understood at all levels. If the will to power is the principle of living things, it follows that nature, at all levels, reveals precisely that aspect of the will: 'the stronger becomes master of the weaker, in so far as the latter cannot assert its degree of independence.'[27]

Such an idea shows more than a certain consonance with the political anthropology proposed by Hobbes, although it is, in many ways, more radical. For Nietzsche, all living things are structured, evidently with growing complexity, on the basis of the will to power, which in Nietzschean terms generally means the will for physical and intellectual supremacy.

> My idea is that every specific body strives to become master over all of space and to extend its force (– its will to power;) and to thrust back all that resists its extension. But it continually encounters similar efforts on the part of other bodies and ends by coming to an arrangement ('union') with those things that are sufficiently related to it: *thus they conspire together for power*. And the process goes on.[28]

In an ontology of this sort, proximity is evidently a fundamental concept and state, as it is through proximity that physical force can be expressed and can become incisive. Translated into political terms, Nietzsche's view clearly has much in common with the idea that space is a fundamental and determining factor in understanding the political dimension, as it is in space that force is deployed and dispelled by the living being that strives to grow. So while self-preservation is the minimal state of that process, where a life form aims for self-preservation when it is helpless to do more, expansion is instead the aim of life forms that are healthy.

There is a point I would like to focus attention on here. In contrast with Darwin and evolutionary theory, Nietzsche stresses how the process he describes of self-preservation and growth is a process that is fundamentally inside living beings, where relationships between wills to power are to be interpreted in terms of energy processes that unfold by means of exchange and, at most, contagion. The external environment, on the other hand, only conditions those processes in minimal terms and ways. Hence, much of what happens is driven by dynamics internal to the organism or, at most, by relational dynamics that arise between organisms, which are interpreted in terms of conflict. Which gives us the turning point for Nietzsche's redefinition of will. Will is not an empty concept that can be freely determined. For Nietzsche, will is always the willing of something. In other words, will is the will to power, which is the growth of the power of one's being.

So let us call this the zero state of nature and of the anthropology adopted by individualistic philosophies. Every zero state, however, presupposes a state of development. But neither Schopenhauer nor Nietzsche appear to have grasped the point, and instead they fix the living being in a state of instinctive and undifferentiated self-perception. Nietzsche, in particular, considered differences as the outcome of fictional cognitive processes. Yet, perhaps the most interesting question comes precisely from individualistic philosophies: How does differentiation occur? How do we move from one to the many? Which in turn leads to another question: Are we really sure that only the spectrum of aggressive or conservative instincts, such as fear, is the key to understanding political and social phenomena?

The short-circuit in individualistic philosophies

The zero state of life is, therefore, apperception, which wills itself and its growth. The idea is ultimately quite simple, and seeks to explain the aggressive and competitive traits to be found as much in nature as in certain aspects of cultural structures. That is the exact theoretical framework adopted by modern philosophy to account for the forces that shape the formation of the political sphere. It is the will that wants everything, as posited by Hobbes, which in Nietzsche becomes the instinct that seeks power at the expense of everything. Indeed, Nietzsche goes further to radicalize the idea, transforming it into outright metaphysical monism. In substance, he conceives of a guiding thread that hypothetically links the will to self-assertion in a seahorse to the will of Dante. From the lowest state of life to the most complex, what drives us is the will to power, organized and ultimately sublimated in different ways.

Through that single principle, a great many fundamental things can therefore be explained. In this regard, it should be stressed how Nietzsche found Dante so extremely interesting, but the seahorse much less so. In other words, his focus is on the multiplicity and variety of ways available to a Dante to express the will to power, rather than on the rather trivial simplicity of ways for expressing the will to power in the natural world. I believe the point should make us stop and think. Why is Nietzsche so fascinated by all the Dantes that history has produced, whereas he shows no interest at all in seahorses? More to the point, does his monism really offer the best insight for understanding what paradigmatically distinguishes Dante from a seahorse, given that they both share the will to power?

Taking his cue from Schopenhauer, Nietzsche argues that the root of apperception is instinctual, and that instinct belongs to the body. Thus, the body cannot be excluded from any analysis of what we are and how we can know. Along the same lines, he holds that emotions and sentiments are none other than a sublimated, if somewhat debilitated and impoverished, form of that same prime instinct – a variation of it that may fool the inexpert eye, but which does not deceive those accustomed to seeking out the essence of things. Yet, the idea of deriving the wider phenomenology of the emotions from the will to power is by no means the most obvious move, producing important implications on the theoretical plane. Those implications deserve particular attention, as they render the world in one single affective dimension.

The underlying idea is that, whether you observe the will to power in a seahorse or in Dante, ultimately there is no difference. A seahorse lives in a less complicated world, from a social point of view, than the world Dante lived in, so we can imagine that the seahorse will express its will to power in more immediate ways. Dante's world, by contrast, was a world of literature and poetry, of love and law, of objectives, disputes and quarrels, of faith and reason. Seahorses use imagination neither in ways as complex as we might nor for imagination's sake. Humans, on the other hand, often make use of the imagination. We create whole new worlds of various levels of complexity and detail, exploring possible variations of actual situations. Nietzsche was well aware of that, and that is why he was much more interested in Dante than in seahorses.

In any case, the point is to determine how justified it is to reduce the complex phenomenology of the emotions we feel to the will to power. Is it really plausible to consider love and hate as two expressions of the same primary instinct? Can sentiments of solidarity, such as sympathy or compassion, similarly be reduced to a variant of the will to power? Nietzsche believed that compassion, in particular, was a sort of affection of the soul, one that substantially weakens vital energy, and as such it should be combated and, if possible, eradicated. Such a belief, however, suffices in itself to invalidate the monist position in relation to emotions because if compassion puts the will to power at risk, then we have two alternatives. The first is to conclude that there are two forms of the will to power, one positive and one negative. That, however, contrasts with Nietzsche's view, which saw the will to power as a neutral force, one that is neither positive nor negative. For him, it simply exists, characterizing all forms of life. The second alternative is to conclude that it is not true that everything is will, given that the will can be weakened by something external to it or, alternatively, something that belongs to it but which is its negative face of sorts, such as compassion.

However we choose to see compassion – Nietzsche was rather ungenerous in considering it always a threat – it is clear that it is difficult to frame within a monist understanding of the will. The same is true of solidarity. Compassion and solidarity are ultimately something totally and profoundly different, resisting all attempts to reduce them to the energy of forces and their variants. That means the world is not as grim as Hobbes, Schopenhauer and Nietzsche describe it, for in describing such a grim and unsettling picture, they were compelled to reduce a plurality of emotions to expressions of a single basic instinct. So let us try, instead, to outline a phenomenology of emotions that is more respectful of what effectively exists.

Phenomenology of the emotions: A broad model

'By emotion [*affectus*] I mean affections of the body by which the body's power of action is augmented or diminished, assisted or restrained, and at the same time the ideas of these affections.'[29] Thus, for Spinoza, in the *Ethics*, emotions relate to the body, inducing modifications that augment or diminish its capacity for action. Emotions modify the body in the sense that they enhance or reduce the capacity for action, which is what ultimately determines self-consciousness and self-knowledge.

In his description, Spinoza is neutral with respect to the emotional component. The human being is essentially a striving for self-preservation. That striving does not necessarily express competition or a struggle to overpower, in the sense that self-preservation can also be achieved in non-competitive ways, implying appetite and desire. Thus, the striving for self-preservation has the structure and form of desire:

> When this endeavor is related to the mind alone, it is called will. But when it is related to mind and body simultaneously, it is called appetite, which accordingly is nothing but a human being's very essence [...]. Then, there is no difference between appetite and desire except that desire is very often attributed to people insofar as they are conscious of their appetite, and therefore it can be defined as follows: *desire is appetite together with consciousness of it*.[30]

Emotions, therefore, belong precisely to a biological structure that desires and seeks its preservation and are capable of steering it towards the enhancement (joy) or diminution (sadness) of its capacity for action. That applies both to the body and the mind, as for Spinoza they are two aspects of the same thing.

The description above gives us one side of the matter. The other side concerns the relationship with external objects. In the metaphysics outlined by Spinoza, external objects are the direct cause of the many different forms that emotions can take. Specifically, love and hatred are none other than joy and sadness associated to the idea of an external cause. Moreover, the essence of the object giving rise to a certain emotion constitutively determines the essence of the emotion:

> For example, the joy arising from object A involves the nature of object A itself, and the joy arising from object B involves the nature of B itself, and therefore these two emotions of joy are different in nature because they arise from causes of a different nature. So too the emotion of sadness arising from one object is different in nature from the sadness arising from a different cause. The same goes for love, hatred, hope, fear, wavering of spirit etc.[31]

In this framework, the imagination plays an important role. It is not only the perception of a thing that determines the modification of the body, the same outcome can be achieved by the image of the thing that comes from the imagination. Images of things (those present but also the images of things past and of possible future things) affect our imagination and are able to modify a body's capacity for action, hence without the need for the effective existence of the thing. Vice versa, the imagination is able to act on an image, as the image, for instance, may be tied to past emotions or memories that depend on different objects. In this case, Spinoza appears to have in mind a sort of affective contagion, whereby a certain emotion can be associated with a certain thing simply because it has already happened to us in the past. Repetition, compulsion and habit, therefore, play a central role.

In Spinoza's phenomenology of emotions, temporality is the medium that enables their passage from one state to another:

> From what we have just said we see what hope, fear, reassurance, despair, relief and remorse are. *Hope is* simply *an inconstant joy arising from the*

image of something in the future or in the past about whose outcome we are in doubt. Conversely, fear is an inconstant sadness which also arises from an image of something that is in doubt. Once the doubt is taken away from these emotions, hope turns into *assurance* and fear into *despair*, i.e. into *the joy or sadness arising from the image of the thing we either feared or hoped for.* Then *relief is joy arising from the image of a thing in the past whose outcome we had been in doubt.* And *remorse is the sadness that is the opposite of relief.*[32]

Thus, the temporal dimension introduces an element of fluidity and of decisive uncertainty in understanding the changes in the state or tone of certain emotions. Alongside time, which is manifested concretely in the capacity to project ourselves forward into the future or back into the past, the imagination is the second element at play in the process of differentiating desire. We are, in fact, capable of imagination in relation to not only ourselves but also what is other to us. We imagine many things in relation to the objects of our love and hate; for example, we imagine the objects of our hate are sad or we imagine things and situations that we know will or would make them sad. Such a condition generally enhances the joy we feel, which is reactive in nature. An equivalent but contrary situation is given when we imagine that an object of our love is experiencing something that brings it joy, and by imagining that specific situation we feel joy in our own turn. Then again, we are also capable of imagining someone else feeling a certain emotion and then feeling, through that act of the imagination, the very same sentiment. Empathy is the primary disposition that allows us to feel how others are feeling and to form affective and rational responses accordant to the context we find ourselves in.

In imagining the objects of our love and hate or ourselves, in turn, as the subjects of love and hate, we feel specific emotions that depend on external causes, past experience or, again, associations made by our imagination. Thus, it happens that we are modified not only by existing objects but also by objects imagined or objects remembered. Imagination and memory therefore fulfil a central function in our capacity to feel emotions and to be modified by them. Memory fulfils a retentive function and modifies what we retain through experience; imagination creates variants of reality by constructing possible scenarios and enables us to attribute emotions and sentiments to human and non-human animals. Spinoza demonstrates very well how imagination and memory are faculties that enrich and complement our emotional life, which is intrinsically varied and relational.

Desire and conflict

We have seen how modern political philosophy has developed largely around the rather wholesale assumption of atomistic individualism. That assumption overturns the Aristotelian perspective in understanding society. Aristotle considered the disposition for sociability as preliminary and foundational with respect to the individualistic dimension. Variations of the theme include the idea for which the concept of 'we' comes before the 'I', and the view that the relationship with the Other is a fundamental component in the formation of personality. We have repeatedly underscored how modern political thought has completely excluded the logic of that idea. That is especially seen in Machiavelli and Hobbes, who both placed radical individualism at the foundation of society, where the interpretive key to understanding society revolves around the 'I' and its will and disposition for desire that is potentially infinite, omnivorous, disgregating and destructive.

That is the idea underpinning Hobbes's description of the state of nature as a (imaginary) dimension in which human beings live submerged by virtually infinite desire. The infinity of desire is obviously a bad thing here, something that humans are called upon to limit if they are to avoid the destructive outcomes it entails. Hobbes takes it on himself to draw that limit in terms of political theory, by imagining a legal stratagem through which individuals give up a part of their freedom in return for the guarantee of survival. The task of the social contract is to guarantee the passage to the civil state and its endurance. It also guarantees the limitation of desire, given that, as we have seen, desire is the core driver of the state of nature. The individual who lives in the state of nature is an individual who by right and in practice places no limit on his or her desire.

Individualistic philosophies hold that the containment of desire is a task to be performed by the 'I', in practice supported by a normative apparatus that facilitates the self-limitation process that is indispensable for the formation of society. It is the agent who chooses to limit his absolute desire by entering into the social contract. Such a process is premissed on a number of assumptions.

First, that the agent is the primary entity; second, that the agent is charged with a desire that is potentially destructive not only for the world around him but also for himself, and as such needs to be limited; and third, that such a limit requires an external apparatus making it both possible and sustainable over time.

The centrality of desire is posited by both Spinoza and Hobbes; the former identifies it as the ontological key to humanity, while the latter considers it a characteristic peculiar to the individual in the state of nature. Whereas Spinoza perfectly understands how self-conscious appetite lies at the heart of nature, and of humanity in particular, Hobbes stresses how it is the keystone underpinning the passage from the individual to the collective dimension, for the purpose of the social contract is to limit the absolute aspects of the power of desire through the introduction of a normative framework external to the agent – which amounts to saying that what the agent is incapable of handling subjectively, through the limitation of the self, can instead be governed through the introduction of objective normative limits from the outside, substantially things like the social contract or a constitutional charter. In a sense, Spinoza was more realistic in his perfect understanding that desire constitutes the condition of possibility for the emotions, which alone would suffice to explain how desire cannot be expunged from humans. Having said that, it is also worthwhile noting how desire, as Spinoza treats it, is not something static in nature or something that exists in itself like an empty vessel. Rather, desire is pervasive and dynamic, and by its very nature necessarily entails the Other, which is essential for its individuation, for desire to become a specific desire.

What individualistic philosophies apparently fail to capture in their account of the dynamics for containing desire is the idea that desire is a process, unfolding through the relationship with the Other. In individualistic philosophies, that Other, in all its possible forms, is generally relegated to a role of mere opposition. In that sense, it is what stands opposed and can cause harm. It is the existence of the Other that leads fear to become the absolute driver of the modern political dimension. Ultimately, the Other is foreign to us, something we encounter in the world and for which it is prudent to conceive of a defence strategy.

Nevertheless, such a separation is problematic for many reasons. Spinoza grasped the root of the problem. Desire is never empty; it is not a mere force. Rather, desire takes on the characteristics of that which is desired, given that it intrinsically relates to the Other. The crucial point, therefore, is to understand how such a necessary relationship unfolds. If we accept the thesis that the Other lies at the core of the structure of the 'I', or the desiring individual, Hegel's explanation of the unfolding of the 'I' as a process would appear better placed to account for all the complexity that nests within the idea.

Beyond individualism: Relationships of recognition

Hegel subverts the terms in which the question is posed in individualistic philosophies, bringing his anthropology back into the Aristotelian fold by considering the human disposition for sociability as an absolute primitive trait. People are therefore predisposed to being sociable because it is in the relationship with the Other that the possibility of the social dimension, and above all the determination of individuality, arises. In other words, for Hegel, without the Other the 'I' cannot exist, as it is precisely in the unfolding of the I-Other relationship that subjectivity is fully constituted.

To begin with, Hegel's theory signifies two things. First, in contrast with what we find in Hobbes, the presence of the Other is shifted from the outside to inside the subject, being its constituent dimension. Second, for Hegel, the subject exhibits a structure that is evidently conflictual. The conflict, however, is not outside the subject, something to be managed, controlled or avoided. The conflict lies in the very heart of the 'I' and is the key to understanding the possibilities for defining its identity and its development.[33] The Other is not what lies outside desire, a real or possible consequence of it; rather, it is the relational dynamics with the Other, inside desire, which enables the 'I' to recognize itself through a process of mirroring and differentiation. In this way, Hegel traces the conflict within the dynamics through which individuality is determined. As Axel Honneth notes,

> The structure of any of these mutual relationships is always the same for Hegel: to the degree that a subject knows itself to be recognized by another subject with regard to certain of its [the subject's] abilities and qualities and is thereby reconciled with the other, a subject always also comes to know its own distinctive identity and thereby comes to be opposed once again to the other as something particular.[34]

The Other is not first and foremost someone to defend ourselves against. The Other is also what enables the 'I' to individuate itself as a subjectivity distinct and separate from the world. It is through the Other that the 'I' has the opportunity to know itself and it is through the Other that the 'I' has the opportunity to differentiate itself from what it itself is not, remaining in itself. Thus, we see how the dimension of otherness is first of all intrinsic to subjectivity. It is also clear how subjectivity is characterized by an intrinsic social disposition – the 'we' has its roots planted deep in the most profound nature of the self. Outside of that disposition, the process of constructing individuality would not be possible. In this sense, the disposition for sociability is primary because the role played by the Other in the constitution of the self is primary.

Hegel is abundantly critical of the framework offered by individualistic philosophies, yet he nevertheless maintains some of the distinctive characteristics of those philosophies, bringing them together in a highly innovative way. Hegel essentially maintains three aspects: conflict, which he reinterprets in an entirely new way; the idea of the social contract, revisited and recast mainly in an empirical sense; and alongside them, the idea of desire understood as a narcissistic and appropriative force, which lies at the heart of the self-formation process through relationships of recognition.

Thus, the disposition for sociability is brought to the core of individuality itself, as is conflict, which becomes an intrinsic element of the process of defining the 'I', of the process of distinguishing the 'I' from the Other by the self and, more generally, of the recognition process as a whole, for it is through conflict that recognition becomes possible. Moreover, it should be added that Hegel considers some sort of form of recognition to be necessary, even before the foundation of the state is stipulated, as recognition and conflict are two aspects of the one process and should be thought of together as determining characteristics of that process. The consideration counts first and foremost for the formation of the 'I', as the 'I' recognizes itself through its conflict with what is Other to the self. The further development of that process then enables the very first bases to be laid for the formation of the legal person and its recognition. Hegel[35] treats intersubjective recognition as the precondition for any form at all of sociality. Without recognition, not only would children never become autonomous subjects but also it would not be possible for them to become part of a social dimension.[36]

If we accept the idea that conflict is part and parcel of recognition relationships, which extend to both the sphere of the formation of the individual and the sphere of the construction of sociality, then the social contract can meaningfully be understood in an empirical key. Such a reading highlights its specific function or utility in fostering civil cohabitation, governed by suitable forms of law and accessible to those individuals who have formalized the concept of legal person. In other words, it is only because recognition enables the formation of the idea of the individual and legal person that the social contract becomes possible and its adoption proves useful. Hegel outlines a precise framework enabling us to see the social contract in different ways, but it also shines a new light on our relationship with property. Humans do not stipulate the social contract in an effort to defend their property, or out of fear of losing it, but rather to be recognized as legal persons holding rights.

In that framework, Hegel also reinterprets fear as an emotion tied directly to recognition. In the social state, the fear human beings feel of losing their property is a superficial fear, an epiphenomenon of a much deeper fear, which is the fear of not being recognized as independent subjects, as legal persons and individuals at one and the same time. Such fear directly touches on identity and is universal in nature. We see it expressed whenever people demand respect and recognition of their fundamental rights, regardless of their capacities and abilities. This is the kind of recognition that Hegel attributes to the legal sphere, encompassing the recognition of human rights.

It is something of a paradox to note how human beings have a need to be recognized as humans, but in truth we only realize the necessity of the recognition process in all those cases in which it fails. That is to say, in cases such as when a child is not loved properly or is abused, where recognition through love fails to be given and the child's personality is left scarred and incomplete. Or in cases where a society does not recognize the legal identity of a person, denying her/him fundamental human rights and mistaking legal recognition for social recognition, where once again it is the identity of that person that is injured. The failure to recognize legal identity is similarly witnessed in the lack of recognition given to immigrants who arrive in the most unlikely ways on Europe's shores, as well as in the lack of recognition of the rights of future generations.

It is a point that Hegel grasped perfectly, but which still today is incredibly tricky to understand, explain and put into practice in public policy. To its credit, the metaphysics of recognition constructed by the German philosopher explains a number of important things. First of all, it explains the construction of the 'I', to which we should attribute the properties of process and not of substance, given that recognition is not an attribute we predicate of a substance, but rather a relationship that emerges from a process between at least two people. Hegel's conception of the form and structure of recognition is of the widest scope, moving from the maximum particularity of the 'I' that recognizes itself in its relationship with the Other, to the maximum generality of the subject that becomes an individual person through relationships made possible by the ethical state. Clearly, a decisive role is played in that process by the formation of the legal sphere, thanks to which the conditions are created for much broader recognition, extending beyond the confines of the family through a process of abstraction and generalization of the person. Such generalization is what makes it possible to effectively approach not only the Other, the entity enabling the 'I' to individuate and objectify itself, but also the idea of the Other, an entity so abstract yet so concrete at the same time, which Herbert Mead called 'the generalized other'.[37]

Mead's work provides Hegel's idea with a concrete basis, supported by empirical evidence from research in the field of psychology. In particular, he identifies relations of play that characterize the life of children as a fundamental element in the self-formation process. As he sees it, that happens in two ways. In the first, children construct their identity through play, by imitating the key figures of reference in their lives. Children assume their behaviours through the introjection of typical traits, which serve a normative function in setting rules and limits. In the second, children play a game based on the capacity to act by imagining the countermoves of adversaries. That development in the capacity for play does not turn on the capacity to imitate, but rather on the capacity to predict the actions of adversaries. In such games, not only is there a conception of the Other but also the understanding of the mind of the Other is a fundamental element for the success of the game.

According to Mead, those same dynamics underpinning the playing of games determine the emergence of society through the notion of the 'generalized other'. In role-playing games, children learn not only to put themselves in another's shoes but also to develop a concept of a separate 'other', capable of acting as an independent subject who pursues specific goals – such as, for example, winning. In other words, children who are capable not only of playing ball but also of playing a ball game show a series of skills – skills concerning rules (those representing the ABC of the game), skills predicting the behaviour of teammates, who presumably, will help them win the match, and finally, skills calculating the behaviour of opponents, who share the same goal but will oppose them in seeking to achieve it. In the case of our ball game, each child will have two generalized others as reference. The first is the team on which they play. Although the team is made up of individual players, the children will learn to treat it as a single entity as, from the point of view of the dynamics of the game, the players act in unison as a single subject, with the team members – the players – working together in search of victory. It is an abstraction that the children learn to make, one which in certain respects is more economical than treating each player as an individual and predicting each of their moves. Then there are the players who belong to the opposing team, which constitutes another generalized other, but of a different kind. The objective is the same, but in pursuing it each team will obviously seek to assert itself over the other, developing its own strategies and a specific game plan. Thus, the opposing team will be another Other, capable of acting as a single subject.

The consolidation of the processes of recognition and abstraction gives rise to those properties typical of the legal sphere, which render the generalized other a subject in the fullest sense, one holding rights and obligations.[38] Alongside the same lines as Hegel, therefore, Mead is now able to overturn the perspective of individualistic philosophies to assert that 'The structure, then, on which the self is built is this response which is common to all, for one has to be a member of a community to be a self.'[39] The structure underpinning the formation of the self is the same structure underpinning relationships of recognition at all levels, as that structure is shared by all members of a community. It follows, therefore, that the community plays a key role in the formation of the self and in shaping, in practice, its construction. The particular other, at a first level, and the generalized other, at a second level, effectively direct the formation of the self as they are the conditions of possibility of the self – respectively on the individual plane, in the loving mother-child relationship, where the child experiences first attachment and then the process of separation, generating anger and frustration, but also identity and individuality, and on the social plane.

The relationship of recognition that structures the mother-child relationship is what enables the bases to be laid for the recognition and integration of the individual in the social sphere. It is interesting how Mead, in reiterating and supporting the point, outlines a topography of the subject by distinguishing between the 'I' and 'me'. The 'I' is a reservoir of instincts; it is what provides the material for the individual, interacting constantly with the 'me', which represents the sphere of normativity, conventions and customs through which the subject relates to the social world from the very start of its conscious life. The constant dialectic between the 'I' and the 'me' highlights how the 'I' constantly attempts to assert its own peculiar qualities to attain recognition from the social context. As such, the 'I' demands the constant 'enlargement' of the 'me' in order to be recognized in all its fullness. That is, when the 'I' exceeds the 'me', or does not coincide with it completely, the need emerges to adjust the generalized other with which the subject interrelates from a normative, ethical and moral point of view, through a process of idealization carried out by the 'I', in which new characteristics are attributed to the generalized other or its existing aspects are modified. In substance, the 'I' imagines a generalized other whose ideal traits it expects will shape future society positively – an idealized Other to which it would like to belong and to which it can refer to regulate its behaviour.[40]

Thus, the 'I' has two fundamental needs, both of which are tied to recognition – the need to be recognized by the community and the need to be recognized for what it is. That generally implies a partial adjustment of some (few or many, as they may be) social norms which the 'I' resists in order to correct them or to introduce new ones. The demand for recognition is, therefore, the mechanism, together with the revision of current ethical-social norms, that drives the greater part of social change. Essentially, the subject demands recognition from the social context in ways that are not general but which reflect her/his own specific individuality. For that to happen, the social context has to positively accommodate a series of adjustments to ethical and moral norms that the subject considers significant.

Thus, Mead proposes a general topography based on at least four elements: the 'subject' (union of the 'I' and 'me'); the 'other', which enters the relationship of recognition by enabling the subject to form, within the bounds of the dualistic relationship, its own identity; the 'generalized other', or the abstract social dimension, whose recognition by the subject is an essential condition for the subject to be recognized in turn as a legal person with rights and duties; and finally, the 'idealized generalized other', which is a regulatory and, at the same time, normative entity of an ideal nature, coinciding with the ethical-normative structure to which the subject is willing to assent in full.

The concept of the idealized generalized other is particularly interesting for our purposes for various reasons. From a metaphysical standpoint, it is a particular entity that serves a regulatory and normative function. More importantly, however, in contrast with the 'me', which is firmly rooted in society and in the cultural stratifications from which it originates, it does not exist. The generalized other reflects the outcome of a correction – the correction the 'I' makes to the 'me' in pursuing its own ends. Hence, it is the way the 'I' corrects the normativity borne by the 'we' in such a way as to steer it in a direction more to its liking. The idealized generalized other is therefore an intrapsychic entity that allows the subject to ideate a projection of the kind of reality in which she would like to live, one exhibiting characteristics partially different from those manifested in reality and which the subject is willing to pursue in action. In that sense, the idealized generalized other is something that at once exists and does not exist, thus exhibiting, by virtue of this duality, a strong regulatory character.

Both Hegel and Mead share the idea that it is by virtue of legal recognition that the passage can be achieved from the concreteness of relationships based on love to subsequent idealizations in which relationships acquire a universal character, via successive processes of abstraction. The legal sphere is what governs the recognition of universal rights and duties, and it is typically a sphere of reason in which emotions have no place. That means that we have learned to recognize and attribute to people – as people, and hence with the highest degree of universality – rights and duties on the basis of a process of universalization and abstraction of the Other.

This peculiarity of the legal sphere, namely the fact of being the pure domain of rationality, explains many things. For example, it explains why in general it is so difficult to impose reason on the general interest. Emotions, as we have seen, are an excellent spur to action; reason, on the contrary, is not always so compelling, and when it is, it is not directly so, which is why it is not unseldom that we draw on emotions to support an intuition of a universal character, which can be explained by reference to reason alone.

The distinction between legal recognition and social recognition is what allows us to formulate the principle of equality on which the modern state is based. On the basis of that distinction, each and every person possesses intrinsic value, and the recognition of that value is what allows us to assert their equality and to recognize their universal rights, regardless of social value. Social value, on the other hand, underpins the recognition of the particular abilities that an individual possesses and which can be measured on the basis of criteria of social relevance. It is legal recognition that makes it possible to attribute universal rights to people as people, regardless of their specific abilities or skills.

Our way of being in the world is therefore structured on the basis of rather complex relationships of recognition, developed roughly along two axes. The first is recognition that lies on the axis of love. In the mother-child relationship, the relationship of recognition is structured through the process of attachment and separation, which is the process that enables the formation of individuality. The second axis, instead, is given by relationships of recognition in the social sphere. Even in this case, recognition should be understood as a dynamic process, structured over two stages: the generalized other and the idealized generalized other. The relationship with the generalized other permits the formation of the legal person and enables the recognition of rights and duties of a universal character, which belong, that is, to the person as a person. It is along this second axis that the process of progressive idealization unfolds, through which each subject develops their social identity, shaped even here by the twin desires of belonging to and distinguishing oneself from the social context. According to Mead, that is because the subject is made up of two impulses, one that drives her/him to assert her/his individuality (the 'I'), and one that drives her/him to adapt to sociality (the 'me'). At the highest degree of idealization, the person is conceived as what has value in and of itself, where such value is grasped through an act of intuition, in a sphere that is the exclusive domain of reason. The (idealized) generalized other is therefore something that is known intuitively, towards which we feel no particular bond or affective attachment. It is an entity that is both individual and universal, to which we attribute universal properties and recognize universal rights and duties. Ultimately, it is a sort of regulatory ideal.

Transgenerationality and recognition

The Hegel-Mead model builds on an understanding of the relational dynamics that characterize all stages of life, and as such it stands clearly opposed to the anthropological model proposed by individualistic philosophies. In doing so, it allows us to situate transgenerationality in both the sphere of the primary, loving relationship between parents and children as well as the sphere of secondary relationships, in particular the legal relationship.

Thus, I will show how transgenerationality is constituted in increasingly complex ways, starting from a biological trace, or physical imprint, marking the transgenerational passage in the parent-child relationship, to arrive at the highest degree of generalization and idealization in the transgenerational relationship uniting diverse generations. That passage, therefore, goes from the greatest concreteness to the greatest idealization, unfolding within the relationship of recognition.

In what was unknown to Hegel in his day, scientific research today is exploring the hypothesis that primary transgenerationality emerges not only from an affective, relational component (as Hegel grasped and psychologists have verified empirically) but that a biological component is involved as well. Dickson and his colleagues[41] have discovered that male subjects exposed to particularly stressful (such as a premature separation from their mothers) or abusive conditions in life, as adults show alterations in the composition of their sperm. Alterations of the same sort have also been found in the sperm of mice subjected to conditions of stress. Then there is the correlation that has been demonstrated to exist between the exposure of children to traumatic events or episodes of severe stress in the earliest stages of development and the manifestation of physical and psychological pathologies.[42] Scientific evidence has also confirmed the transgenerational transmission of such pathologies.[43]

As such, Dickson and his colleagues decided to look for physical traces evidencing the correlation between a traumatic event and a psychological disorder, which they then found in the significant decrease in two particular types of cytoplasmic RNA contained in sperm (miRNAs 449 and 34). The exact function of those micro RNAs is not known, but what we do know is that they are small fragments of RNA that adversely regulate gene expression, interfering with normal RNAs and inhibiting the transformation of the information they carry into proteins. By changing the destiny and function of cells, the micro RNAs determine the onset of pathological processes and are involved in the proliferation or death of those cells.

Dickson and his colleagues examined the levels of micro RNAs 449 and 34 in a sample of adult males, who had donated sperm to a fertility clinic. To begin with, the volunteer donors were asked to answer an Adverse Childhood Experience (ACE) questionnaire, through which their exposure as children to episodes of severe stress or trauma was measured. A score of 4 on the ACE questionnaire was considered the risk threshold indicating forms of abuse in the life of the child. The researchers then analysed a sample of sperm from donors who scored 4 or more on the questionnaire. The study found that in all cases, subjects with an ACE score equal to or greater than 4 showed anomalous levels of micro RNA. The finding led them to conclude that severe stress factors or trauma are capable of modifying male sex cells. Moreover, the study on mice found that the modification is passed on in the spermatozoa of offspring, thereby affecting more than one generation.

From a more general perspective, such research shows how the most basic building blocks of transgenerationality are found in biology, encompassing not only the mother-child relationship, as Hegel believed in his outline of the structure of recognition, but also reaching an even deeper level in the father-son relationship. Signs of trauma are passed on from father to son via genetics, shaping genetics by leaving their trace. Thus, we have the first form of biological transgenerationality, a trace that binds generations physically, along the paternal line. Here, the mother cannot compensate for what is lacking from the father; she cannot erase the trace.

The mother-child relationship, which Hegel identified as the constituent moment of the relationship of recognition, bears witness to the evolution of the transgenerational bond – the mother-child bond is a bond that is both profoundly physical and psychological. It is structured on the dynamics of attachment and separation, making it a conflictual bond for the child, who suffers the experience of separation from the mother, as he learns to perceive her as an object that is not at his total disposal, which elicits ambivalent sentiments in the child.

Hegel correctly related what for us is the second form of transgenerationality to the dynamics of recognition. In the transgenerational bond between mother and child – a bond which, to begin with, is experienced as a state of oneness – what ties the two is both a physical and a psychological bond. In turn, what I have called social personality is rooted in two aspects that Hegel theorized as legal recognition and social recognition. The theory I will attempt to prove in the following chapters is that in the legal sphere, the transgenerational bond should be grasped, as Hegel suggests, by an act of mere intuition. That does not mean that transgenerationality does not exist, as we are often led to conclude, but rather that, in contrast with what happens in primary transgenerationality, it is not accessible by means of any particular visible trace. To grasp and understand its nature, we need to take a different approach. Secondary transgenerationality finds its most typical form of expression in legal recognition. One of the steps that leads to such recognition lies in determining what the entity we call 'future generation' is. As we will abundantly see, future generations constitute an indispensible component in the fulfilment of transgenerational social actions.

In practice, we are beginning to understand quite well the ontology of primary transgenerationality. It is constituted by primary sentiments such as love and hate, by primary relationships such as the mother-child relationship, and it is physically conveyed, as in the case of alterations in the micro RNAs of men subjected at an early age to stress or major abuse. The typical characteristic of primary transgenerationality is that it is marked by perceptible and decipherable traces. It is the outcome of strong, visible, concrete ties, such as family ties, and leaves its mark on the mind, the body and actions, for which it is not hard to recognize. In general, we readily concede that family relationships are characterized by self-evident transgenerational bonds – something we recognize in various ways at the legal level, for instance through succession, which secures the line of inheritance from parents to children, or in the duty of care that parents have towards children and vice versa.

Instead, what specifically characterizes secondary transgenerationality is the fact that it does not leave immediately perceptible traces at either the emotional or physical level. But it does leave many traces, as we shall see, on the social fabric that a society develops over time. Those traces are important and often rich in meaning, even if we generally tend to neglect them or mistake them. Such mistakes, however, give rise to no few problems.

3

Metaphysics

Transgenerationality is a bond that obliges us to plan the future, which means taking the future into consideration when shaping the present. Planning the future draws on two orders of knowledge: what we know of the present and what we can anticipate and imagine of the future. Thus, there is a modal dimension to transgenerationality, in the sense that the transgenerational bond implies the need to imagine possible worlds and their structures, characteristics and axiological and normative frameworks.

The capacity to imagine and plan ahead is an identifying characteristic of humans. This distinguishes human animals from non-human animals, which although extremely effective in the way they use and conceive space, lack the capacity to project themselves in time – they do not, for instance and perhaps most notably, think of death. Therefore, it is the faculty of the imagination that enables us to project ourselves as a species in relation to the passing of generations, and hence the transgenerational structure of the species. The imagination acts as an intermediary between our perception of the outside world and our capacity to organize it and anticipate it in a modal sense. This comes into play when the emotions – the direct cause behind primary transgenerationality – are diminished or entirely lose their capacity as a stimulus.

Having posed the problem of transgenerationality and explained the reasons suggesting why it should be addressed from a philosophical viewpoint, and having outlined the anthropological context in which transgenerational bonds find their reason for being, in this chapter we will explore the metaphysical framework underpinning a transgenerational theory of society. If we put aside the cheap rhetoric that leads politicians and institutions to say that society needs to protect future generations and then take little to no action about it in terms of substantial decision-making, it becomes clearer how the nature and modes of transgenerational relationships conceal a tangle of problems knotted around questions of justice and normativity. The crucial point, as I see it, is that to untangle the mess, it is first of all necessary to understand the underlying metaphysics – a metaphysics which is particularly interesting and complex, and which concerns several levels and various components of social reality. To do so, this inquiry is divided into four categories: agents, actions, emotions and faculties. Then it attempts to answer questions concerning the identity and nature of transgenerational agents; the nature and structure of the actions they carry out; and finally to analyze the faculties that support and enable transgenerationality.

Agents

The aim of the considerations that follow is to understand (1) the identity of agents as bearers of transgenerationality and (2) the structure of transgenerational actions. As we have seen, primary transgenerationality poses no particular problems, as its agents are identified by family ties. They are mothers and fathers, grandparents, children and grandchildren – people tied in some way by a biological bond. Given that it is a bond that emerges through a relationship, to exist the transgenerational bond requires at least two agents constituting the transgenerational relationship. Thus, the agents of primary transgenerationality are tied by a biological and affective bond and moved by emotions such as, above all, love, care and friendship. Spinoza taught that at the root of individuality there is the Other, in the form of desire. In relation to the Other, the parental figure in the first instance, children experience a relationship of dependency, marked by love and by need. Any state of need carries the potential for an aggressive response in the event that the state of need is not satisfied or simply postponed.

Fundamentally, that implies two things. The first implication is that there is an ambivalence that marks the deeper nature of the human being. Whenever we place a limit on the limitlessness of desire, love reveals its aggressive, conflictual and potentially destructive side. It is at that point that the phenomenology of the emotions takes shape. The second implication concerns the asymmetrical nature of the transgenerational relationship, where in the case of primary transgenerationality, the asymmetry lies in the direction of the parents towards the child. Generalizing this point, we can argue that transgenerationality is consciously dealt with by the agent in the relationship with the capacity to steer the relationship in terms of rationality and awareness. It is the mother who contains the child's desire and gives shape to otherness by acting as an otherness that is given and taken, such that the child learns there is a time for waiting and a time for presence. In doing so, the child learns to modulate and handle desire, and to perceive herself as a separate and distinct individuality. It is the mother who places and moves the boundaries, as it is the mother who more or less distinctly understands the reasons and dynamics of the mother-child relationship, which is specifically a transgenerational relationship.

Where there is a tie there is a bond. Where there are ties and bonds there are also conventions and norms governing them. The normativity of primary transgenerationality is governed in its very general and public aspects by family law, and within each specific family by the parental figures of reference. Hegel structures the relationship of recognition starting from the mother figure, but the transgenerational relationship obviously involves all the various agents who play a multiplicity of roles in the life of the child – affective, educational and symbolic roles that change and vary as children grow and continue their development. The transgenerational character of the parental relationship emerges from both an affective and an educational point of view, as parents have a duty of care towards their children, from both a material and moral perspective, until they reach adulthood.

That the parent-child bond is a bond of a transgenerational nature – not just a parental nature – means that it is a type of relationship that obliges parents to plan the future of their children. To begin with the obligation is asymmetrical and tipped towards the parents, who are the main agents of transgenerationality, in the sense that the affective and educational responsibility for their children falls on them. In the longer term, however, the relationship tends to balance itself out and become equal, and if all the agents of the relationship live long enough, there will come a time when the transgenerational duty of care will pass from the parents to the children, where the relationship of care is inverted (see Figure 1).

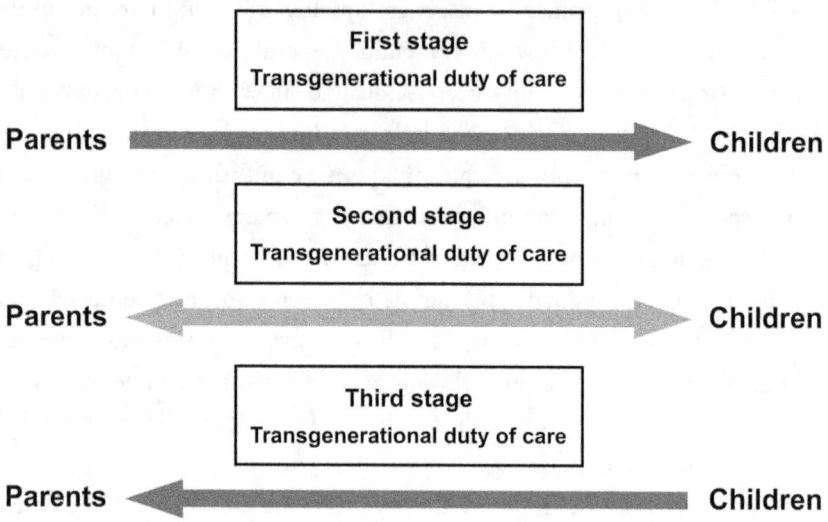

Figure 1 Primary transgenerationality: the parental relationship.

The transgenerational relationship is identified by a rational component as well as an emotional and affective component. That is true starting from biological transgenerationality, which is handled exclusively or predominantly, depending on the stages of the relationship, by the more rational agents in the relationship. It is important to stress how the transgenerational relationship exists, how it can be managed and how in practice it is managed by one or more agents vicariously, meaning that it can be managed by one or more agents without the other agents involved being aware of it.

So far we have termed primary transgenerationality as biological transgenerationality, but it can also exist in the absence of any biological bond, as evidenced in cases of adoption or fostering without kinship. That means that the biological bond may be a sufficient condition but not a necessary condition for the formation of the primary transgenerational bond, as it can be replaced by an affective bond of non-biological origin. From a legal point of view, primary transgenerationality of non-biological origin takes on the same legal structure as the biological transgenerational relationship as a relationship based on love, care, education; on the responsibility of the parent towards the child, to begin with, and later of the child towards the parent; and as seen in Chapter 2, on the progressive recognition of otherness, a process that makes the formation of personal identity possible.

Present and absent agents

Agents who act within the legal space identified and described by Hegel are not just single individuals. Often they can be institutional agents, that is, persons who act on behalf or on account of somebody or something that invests them with the powers to make decisions and take action. Such agents are not bound by a transgenerational bond based on a biological bond or, for the most part, on an affective bond. Rather, the transgenerational bond is developed within a legal and normative framework that both requires it and makes it possible. The point leads us to consider relational forms that are extremely broad in terms of the sheer number of agents involved as well as their extension in time. They are transgenerational relationships developed by political organizations, such as states or meta-states, or bodies that overarch states and meta-states. Historically, there has been an overriding tendency to consider states as political institutions that arise for the purposes of defence. One of the chief tasks of Leviathan, for instance, is to defend the citizens who found it and keep it alive, along with their property and the territory they occupy.

Nevertheless, there is another no less important characteristic identifying the nature of the state, which in Hobbes's conception of it is that it is indeconstructible. Thus, it is potentially destined to last, by law at least, forever. Hobbes argues the point on grounds that are entirely theoretical in nature, but it must be said that more practical arguments are by no means lacking. Wars and wide-scale death are necessary to deconstruct a state, but things are different for a nation. Unless it were possible to completely eliminate the deeper culture that constitutes collective memory, ultimately it is probably safe to say that nations are indeconstructible, which suffices to show that both political theory and practice confirm Hobbes's arguments. If that is true, the fact that states can potentially last indefinitely calls for serious philosophical reflection on its implications.

First of all, it should be noted that such awareness is firmly rooted in the sphere of political practice. This is seen in the way governments take such indeconstructibility for granted, especially in steering economic decisions, where they generally exploit the transgenerational bond to their advantage; whereas, as we will see, they almost never display such sensitivity when it is a matter of considering the consequences of policy decisions that imply a reliance on transgenerationality.

Hegel and Mead identified the figure of the generalized other and the legal space that makes it possible as the framework of reference for the confrontation with 'otherness as such'. Here, otherness as such represents secondary transgenerationality, substantially in the sense that it stands for a kind of absent agent, or an agent that is not imbued with the same sort of presence or reality as the agents on the other end of the transgenerational relationship and action. This is an important difference with respect to the structure of primary transgenerationality, where the agents are all actively present, albeit in different ways, in the transgenerational relationship. In contrast, secondary transgenerationality shows a peculiar structure, where the agents on one end of the relationship are characteristically absent, while those on the other end are not only present but also in practice make all the decisions, thereby assuming, in theory at least, all the responsibility.

So let us look at and determine the characteristics identifying this 'Other' who in practice is mostly absent (as in the case of future generations) or otherwise present (as in the case of agents who are excluded from the right to vote). What emerges, to begin with, is how the concept of abstract otherness, which stands on one end of the transgenerational relationship, envisages at least two variants, where the Other may be scoped into the political space in which the transgenerational agent acts, or it can be scoped out of the political space in which the transgenerational action is carried out.

The differences, as with the consequences in terms of political action, are evident if democratic systems are considered. Such systems produce governments that, more than in others, require the approval of voters to exist. That approval is expressed here and now, in that it is measured with a certain frequency and over a rather limited time span. Moreover, such time spans are becoming shorter and shorter due to new technologies that enable the pulse of voters to be taken regularly and outside the scope of standardized practices. Such electoral moods, however, almost never correspond to the formation of consolidated and articulated opinions, resulting in a magmatic flow of beliefs and views that complicate the structuring of long-term policy action. As such, the prevalent tendency in democracies, due to the structure itself of democratic systems, is to consider the transgenerational bond as something that can easily be overlooked – future generations do not vote, after all, and young people who have not reached adulthood cannot vote yet – or as a sign of an irresolvable problem.

Building and maintaining popular approval is generally difficult to reconcile with protections for secondary transgenerationality. That is because the agents to be protected fall, on the whole, into two categories: those enfranchised to vote, who therefore can exercise forms of political pressure through the ballot box; and those who, for any number of reasons, are not enfranchised to vote and therefore can exercise no such form of pressure. In short, democratic systems revolve around the logic of *'I vote' therefore I exist*, thereby indirectly endorsing a situation in which those who have no right to vote also have no right to representation. Therefore, voters can participate through representation mechanisms in the debate and determination of policy action, whereas non-voters, being absent through their non-entitlement to the franchise, merely suffer the consequences. That does not mean we should do away with our democratic systems. Rather, it means that, given the intrinsic dependency of the elected on their voters, democracies need to be governed by a more attentive and precise normativity, especially in relation to matters that concern 'absent agents'. For absent agents are not inexistent agents; rather, they are agents that for one reason or another, which itself is stipulated and therefore can be reviewed, have no right to have their opinion represented in some way. And what might seem to be, all things considered, a negligible side effect of the structure of the democratic system is revealing itself to be particularly burdensome, especially in the long term, due to the dramatic effects it is revealing.

It would appear useful, therefore, to look deeper into the question of absent agents. To begin with, at least four types of agents can be identified. If a certain political space x (a state or meta-state) is taken as a reference, there will be: (1) those who find themselves outside the political space of x because they are, for example, citizens of another state that is not x; (2) those who find themselves outside of x because they are not yet citizens of x (for instance, those who have applied for citizenship but have yet to see it granted to them); (3) those who are outside of x because, although they are citizens of x, they have not yet acquired the right to vote because they are minors; and (4) those for whom it may be assumed that one day they will be part of x but at the moment, at time t, they have yet to be born.

It is essential to bear this distinction in mind, as it highlights a grey area in the representativeness of democratic systems, covering all those agents who are entitled to no form of representation at all, or entitled only to partial representation, but who find themselves having to carry out and, in many cases, bear the brunt of decisions taken in the name of those who have the means to be represented, and hence can exercise some form of power. To put it another way, the problem we need to face, and one that generally appears to be underestimated in importance, concerns the fact that a great number of decisions taken regularly by democratic governments entail more or less direct consequences for people who cannot vote and therefore do not enjoy full political representation.

Now, while we can assume that 'citizens of neighbouring states' – in this example, citizens of states neighbouring x – presumably are entitled to some form of representation in their own states and hence are represented by their governments (thus shifting the issue to the problem of justice between states and global justice),[1] the question of future generations is markedly more complex. Indeed, future generations are absent agents in the supreme – agents who do not exist and who cannot be consulted or called to question. Ultimately, they are merely a rhetorical expedient to talk about the future. But more specifically, such absent agents cannot be attributed rights and duties.

The point that transgenerational actions are distinguished by the fact that they endure over time and that they are performed by agents remote in time has been established. It has also been established that, in transgenerational actions, the agents involved have an asymmetrical power of action, as it is only the agents on one end of the relationship who effectively have the power to act. As I have repeatedly stressed, the power of action renders possible consequences that in many cases can be quite major. Agents on the other end of the transgenerational relationship instead find the action imposed on them, without any power or possibility to decide on the action, to influence it or to restructure it. Thus, it is in that sense that we speak of an absent agent from an ontological point of view. Nevertheless, such absence does not correspond to an empty space or simple inexistence because if that second end of the transgenerational relationship were not afforded some sort of reality, then transgenerational actions would not be possible, or they would make no sense, or it would be pointless to carry them out.

Of the four types of absent agent identified above, the first three can attain some form of representation in the event that certain conditions change, or they can acquire representation over the course of time. That is not the case, however, for the fourth type of agent, or future generations. Here we are faced with an absent agent in the supreme – an intrinsically vague agent who, paradoxically, in contrast with younger generations who have no right to vote only because of their young age, may never even come into existence. Thus, it is important to understand exactly what we are referring to when we talk of future generations.

What we are talking about when we talk of (future) generations

The concept of 'generation' can be understood in at least two different ways, each implying a different political collocation and, analogously, a different political effect. The first acceptation, which I shall call 'regulatory', was outlined in its most well-known formulation by Immanuel Kant in his *Political Writings*. The second acceptation, which I shall call 'conservative', is drawn from political practice.

Here I will show how, as much as the Kantian acceptation is preferable both ethically and in practice, especially as concerns long-term considerations, in the everyday world it is almost always the conservative acceptation that wins out. I will also demonstrate how adopting one or the other acceptation is necessary in practice, as taking a stance one way or the other is what permits the future to be represented – something that, if we want to describe and organize social reality, cannot be avoided. Further, I will show how the choice of acceptation poses the material conditions and limits within which the future can effectively come about. In other words, leaning towards the regulatory acceptation rather than the conservative acceptation of future generations brings about a substantial difference in the social reality that follows.

In part, Kant was perfectly right to claim that the possibility for humankind to better itself depends on the assumption that future generations are a regulatory ideal – 'But how is it possible to have history *a priori*? The answer is that it is possible if the prophet himself occasions and *produces* the events he predicts.'[2] That amounts to conceiving of future generations, or their existence, as a regulatory ideal, a goal it is necessary to strive towards, even through the modelling of the present. That is, it makes a substantial difference to think that the world, taken as the set of resources and events that make it up, exists to be utilized in the here and now, rather than to think it exists and should continue to exist independently of our understanding of it now and of our intensive exploitation of it. In that sense, future generations represent the projection of an ideal, while at the same time indicating the relative assumption of responsibility to ensure the continued existence over time of the world and the social reality that makes the life of individuals possible.

Kant's idea is that the transgenerational relationship comes before and completes the individual, who by nature is limited for at least two reasons: (1) human beings have relatively limited time at their disposal – their lifetime – in which in some way they have to retrace all the stages in the formation of themselves as individual from the start; and (2) the human dimension is marked by an 'unsocial sociability', one that is intimately conflictual. By 'unsocial sociability' Kant means the tendency of human beings to come together in society while constantly resisting society, driven by an overriding propensity for individualism. Such instincts reveal the dual nature of humans, who on the one hand are sociable but on the other are wild and individualistic:

> Man has an inclination to *live in society*, since he feels in this state more like a man, that is, he feels able to develop his natural capacities. But he also has a great tendency to *live as an individual*, to isolate himself, since he also encounters in himself the unsocial characteristic of wanting to direct everything in accordance with his own ideas. He therefore expects resistance all around, just as he knows of himself that he is in turn inclined to offer resistance to others. It is this very resistance which awakens all man's powers and induces him to overcome his tendency to laziness. Through the desire for honour, power or property, it drives him to seek status among his fellows, whom he cannot *bear* yet cannot *bear to leave*.[3]

It is precisely by observing the characteristic duplicity of human nature that Kant introduces a useful point for our purposes here, which is interesting, paradoxically, because it is a point that is intrinsically unacceptable. The general line of Kant's thinking is that while human beings want concord, nature – which ultimately knows better than humans what is good for the species – wants discord and adversity, as it is precisely discord that drives humans to bring the best out of themselves. Adversity is a store of particularly creative power, which is what makes it possible to give shape and force to life. Thus, society is an arrangement permitting the maximum discord and the widest order in living together because it ensures the possibility of the greatest antagonism within the greatest freedom. Moreover, adversity is what allows nature to fulfil its course by developing human capacities to the fullest. This is the central point of Kant's insight: nature works to bring about the best, permitting human beings to fulfil all their potentialities over time. The generational legacy constitutes both the remnant and material for that process, while human beings represent the means for it to unfold.

In an effort to sum up, from Kant's perspective, the transgenerational passage is one of growth, teleologically driven for the better. If that is possible, it is because nature fosters the unsocial sociability of humans in such a way that adversity becomes the driver of the moral and civil development of humankind. Which is to say humans achieve their best in spite of themselves by virtue of a sort of trick of reason operated by nature. Since it is nature that determines the design, humans develop it largely unawares.

In this framework, Kant grasps the centrality of time. It is over time that we give shape to things and come to fully understand them. Nevertheless, the time we have at our disposal as individuals is, all things considered, short. Human beings, as social animals, need vast lengths of time, much longer than what nature has granted them. Thus, it becomes central to acquire awareness and the capacity to steer human development over time. Given that it would seem that humans cannot take on such steering activity, Kant introduces an external element to his design of things to help bring about what the human mind is evidently incapable of doing:

> Reason, in a creature, is a faculty which enables that creature to extend far beyond the limits of natural instinct the rules and intentions it follows in using its various powers, and the range of its projects is unbounded. But

reason does not itself work instinctively, for it requires trials, practice and instruction to enable it to progress gradually from one stage of insight to the next. Accordingly, every individual man would have to live for a vast length of time if he were to learn how to make complete use of all his natural capacities; or if nature has fixed only a short term for each man's life (as is in fact the case), then it will require a long, perhaps incalculable series of generations, each passing on its enlightenment to the next, before the germs implanted by nature in our species can be developed to that degree which corresponds to nature's original intention. And the point of time at which this degree of development is reached must be the goal of man's aspirations (at least as an idea in his mind), or else his natural capacities would necessarily appear by and large to be purposeless and wasted.[4]

If such a principle should indeed be the case, then happiness, so to speak, will come at the end of the process:

What remains disconcerting about all this is firstly, that the earlier generations seem to perform their laborious tasks only for the sake of the later ones, so as to prepare for them a further stage from which they can raise still higher the structure intended by nature; and secondly, that only later generations will in fact have the good fortune to inhabit the building on which a whole series of their forefathers (admittedly, without any conscious intention) had worked, without themselves being able to share in the happiness they were preparing.[5]

Kant's words are revelatory. Earlier generations *seem* to pursue their laborious work for the benefit of later generations, to the extent to which nature accomplishes its design. Hence it is not human beings who organize to achieve that end, which ultimately transcends them, but rather nature that seeks the perfectionment, through a very long-term process, of human nature.

The problem, however, lies precisely in this last step. If nature does not in fact perform such a regulatory function, then the transgenerational relationship falls apart – which is indeed what largely happens, as demonstrated by the conservative use of the concept. In contrast with Kant's belief, let us suppose that, beyond the preservation of primary transgenerationality, nature has no tendency to foster secondary transgenerationality. In other words, suppose that nature as such is clearly indifferent to secondary transgenerationality. It would follow that – granting the general validity of the Kantian assumption

– we would need to find a way to commit ourselves to the recognition, affirmation and protection of secondary transgenerationality through a series of shared and acknowledged social practices and norms. The idea is that if nature is not intrinsically purposed to guarantee the protection of secondary transgenerationality, then it is us humans who have to find a way to achieve such an end.

That nature shows no sign of having among its objectives the safeguarding of secondary transgenerationality is evidenced by political action, or more precisely, governmental action, which in practice is predominantly conservative in its use of the concept of future generation, especially in democratic systems. Such a conservative use of the concept is characteristically reflected in how political action focuses primarily on the maintenance of political and social approval, protecting the interests of people entitled to vote. In this context, the concept of future generation serves to enable the fulfilment of the needs of present generations. For instance, in contrast to Kant, the concept serves to ensure that what is undertaken by a certain generation will be brought to term by another generation, without the latter, however, being taken effectively into consideration when the original decision is made. For example, the repayment of a debt contracted by a certain generation in a certain historical moment by subsequent generations at a later time.

Another characteristic of the conservative use of the concept is that the role and function of future generations in society is simply ignored altogether, meaning that societies and their governments act *as if* future generations did not exist or *as if* the existence of future generations were not necessary to guarantee the existence of social reality. Or again, on the one hand, they assume the existence of future generations for the accomplishment of a certain political or social goal, such as when debts are contracted to improve the quality of life of citizens living in a certain historical context or at a certain time, but on the other, when it comes to considering the rights of the entity permitting those debts to be contracted, they simply ignore the question by considering the entity to be inexistent.

Yet future generations fulfil a dual function. On the one hand, they allow social organizations to perform actions of extended duration over time, which therefore can only be pursued by postulating the existence of those future generations. Such actions can only be planned and undertaken if it is assumed that a certain entity that does not yet exist, but which could exist (i.e. an entity with potential existence but that has no actual existence at a certain time t), will in fact be able to take over, and ultimately bring to term, a certain action. On the other hand, future generations represent for societies and for the generations living in a certain span of time a regulatory ideal on the basis of which to determine the content of their actions.

Generational time

Turning to the question of time, what concept of time can we refer to when we talk about generations and future generations?

The ideal snapshot of a society at time t shows the coexistence of various generations, each with its own needs and demands, where those needs will be represented by the political action of a government at time t. Wilhelm Dilthey grasped the point when he stressed how the matter of generations implies a sort of dual temporality – an external time, so to speak, that links the passing of generations, and an internal time within each generation, which characterizes a generation as such and therefore distinguishes it from others. Each generation, Dilthey observed, is characterized by its own internal time, which makes comparisons with the time of other generations troublesome.[6] In other words, Dilthey shifts the attention from the problem of the mathematical quantifiability of generations (their measurement in terms of time) to their qualitative experience. From that perspective, what counts is the time lived, or the time-interval lived by each generation, which distinguishes and identifies the generation itself.

The idea of intragenerational temporality is crucial for understanding the conservative use of the concept of generation. According to such an idea, within the same chronological time live different generations that occupy different generational times at the same instant t, and which will live through different generational times over the time span $t \ldots tn$, or the time lived by a certain generation. Clearly, that permits those who belong to the same generational time to share the same world and show a certain permeability, whereas there will be no permeability of world vision among those who belong to different generations, as the idea is that they share different generational times.⁷ Here, what prevails is the dimension of contemporaneity, or that of being contemporaneous with.

Dilthey's observations help us frame an important point. If it is true, as Hegel suggests, that the relationship with the Other is at the heart of individual and social development, it is also true that, except in the case of primary transgenerationality, the Other is predominantly of generational contemporaneity. In other words, the relationship with the Other shows a preferential tendency to crystallize in the dimension of contemporaneity, where the Other consists of other selves who live in my same age, sharing the contemporaneity that makes up each generational time.

The observation allows us to develop another equally important point, which is that the question of transgenerationality cannot be reduced to the calculability of time, or the temporal cycle marking the life of each generation. As Karl Mannheim observes, to frame the question of transgenerationality in the right context, a broader, more complex framework needs to be taken into account:

> It is a complete misconception to suppose, as do most investigators, that a real problem of generations exists only in so far as a rhythm of generations, recurring at unchanging intervals, can be established. Even if it proved impossible to establish such intervals, the problem of generations would nevertheless remain a fruitful and important field of research.⁸

In other words, it is not a matter of identifying a time-interval marking the passage of generations – that is not the point. Rather, the point is to understand that generations are tied up with time in a very singular and peculiar way. Indeed, generations are linked to a conception of temporality that is far from banal. As we said, time in relation to generations is of two different types: a time internal to generations, which identifies the generation as such, and a time external to generations, providing the thread that ties the different generations together. Time, or rather one or more time units, is what determines the identity of a generation, just as it determines the possibility of the passage from one generation to another. Without time, generations would not exist and they would not exist in the way they do.

But given such premisses, what is a generation? To try and explain what they are, let us first look at what generations *are not*.

What a generation is not (and what it is)

In addressing the question, a helping hand comes from sociology. Karl Mannheim starts by distinguishing generations from concrete groups. The unity of a generation is not a particular bond that materializes in the formation of concrete groups, along the lines of associations, families or communities of like thinkers, even though it can happen that a generation, say the generation that gave rise to the 1968 student movement, can give rise to a concrete group. Mannheim treats the generational bond, or intragenerational bond, as a simple bond that is different from that which unites the members of a group. Concrete groups are made up of individuals in flesh and blood. Their concreteness is given by the most various of factors, such as physical vicinity or the sharing of certain spaces or locations, or by the concreteness of sharing certain experiences of particular significance. Alongside concrete groups, there exist social formations of people who exhibit a shared purpose or goal. In this case, sharing is not a matter of location but of goals or objectives, and it can exist even when the bond made possible by the sharing of physical space disappears.

Concrete groups and social formations, therefore, offer a clear example of what generations are *not*. People who belong to one and the same generation on the whole do not choose goals to share, just as they do not choose the types of bonds that unite them. Rather, they share elements that in a certain sense are accidental, yet they are rather robust. Hence people who belong to one and the same generation share certain things. The difficulty lies in understanding exactly what they are.

To explain the point, Mannheim likens generations, or more specifically, generational membership, to class membership: 'Although the members of a generation are undoubtedly bound together in certain ways, the ties between them have not resulted in a concrete group. How, then, can we describe and understand the nature of the generation as a social phenomenon?'[9] That nature is to be identified in the nature of a bond that is certainly real, even though it is of a different nature to the bond uniting individuals who belong to groups or associations. It could, then, be supposed that individuals belong to a generation in the same way that people belong to a social class, or a certain economic and power structure.

Mannheim argues that while it is true that the alternation of life and death is obviously a necessary condition for the alternation of generations, at the same time it is not a sufficient condition to individuate the identity of a generation. In short, the biological cycle is certainly a necessary condition for there to be a passage of generations, but it is also true that the fact that different generations can be identified does not depend on the biological cycle. Instead, it requires something extra, or more precisely, it requires a social and historical context that determines membership to one generation rather than another, given that, as we have observed, generations are not identified by a neutral temporality, but instead by a temporality with historical and social connotations:

> Were it not for the existence of social interaction between human beings – were there no definable social structure, no history based on a particular sort of continuity, the generation would not exist as a social location phenomenon; there would merely be birth, ageing, and death.[10]

And that is why to understand what a generation is, it is necessary to refer to the qualitative dimension of time.

In this sense, location is what limits and at the same time gives shape. Every location, by its nature, identifies and excludes – it identifies a certain number of facts and events that are relevant for people who are born in a certain range of years, and excludes many more again. Therefore, when we speak of generations, or divide up humanity into a stream of generations, a few elements need to be borne in mind. First, nature is characterized by the coexistence of life and death; second, there has to be a culture and a history that have meaning for the life of people; and finally, memory has to be both preserved as well as lost, as it is that process that concretely identifies the biological rhythm of birth and death. Basically, the pattern is this: some individuals enter the social world, inherit memories and form their own experiences shaped by a certain culture, while others leave the world, inevitably taking with them a part of those and other memories. In that way, the threads of memory continue to be woven and intertwined, albeit not without interruptions and discontinuities.

Here it is also important to focus attention on the structure of temporality, which in this framework becomes incomparably richer. If we assume the validity of Dilthey's distinction between objective time and subjective time, then it makes sense to argue for the idea that generational identification interacts with the life stage lived by each individual. The same experience – for instance the student revolution of 1968 – in all likelihood will have a different meaning and value for different people experiencing it, for a young student, say, or a pensioner, as the event – in this case the series of events – will presumably impact people's lives in different ways. Thus, 1968 will have had a certain meaning for twenty year olds and another completely different meaning for their parents. It is that alternation of entering and leaving the stream of history, combined with the social make-up, the cultural dimension and the flow of history itself that impacts on personal time, giving rise to spontaneous groupings, which are what we call 'generations'.

More can be said, however, about the internal bonds of a generation. It is obvious that differences exist within the same generation, which are grasped in greater detail the more we take into consideration. Nevertheless, in many ways it is fairly clear how such differences and even antitheses are only possible against a certain backdrop, which is given by the union of individual time and historical time. A certain historically connotated time is what creates the backdrop in which individual times and experiences are interwoven. That backdrop lays the bases generally for the characterization of generations and in more detail for specific, individual bonds within the different generations. The context that gives generations their unity is what makes it possible for that unity to be inhabited by a broad spectrum of positions that tend to agglomerate around polarities.

Future generations: A metaphysical inquiry

To develop this part of my argument more effectively, it will be useful to return once more to Woody Allen's quip and what I called the 'common-sense argument'. It is perfectly self-evident that future generations cannot have done anything for those who live, work or do not work, suffer or rejoice, retire or are barred from retirement in the here and now. Given that democracies concern themselves primarily with the immediate gain of their citizens, it is clear that any discussion of future generations will sound rather quaint, at least when brought onto the plane of the preservation of power and ordinary government practice. Taking an interest in future generations does not win support, which means it does not fuel power or help maintain what has been accomplished. So *cui bono*?

There are some good counterarguments to the common-sense argument. One is that it can easily be shown that it is false that future generations have never done anything for us. As illogical as it may seem that something or somebody who does not exist could have done something for somebody who does exist in space and time, we can demonstrate the opposite, for in social reality as we know it, future generations have the property of agency, which means they do things in and as future generations. Their capacity as agents is important, as it allows social reality to exist for an extended length of time, which is why it should be considered with due attention.

Taking a closer look at the matter, how can somebody who does not exist – or does not exist in the conventional sense of the term as having a form of existence determined by space and time – have done something for those who exist in flesh and blood, and as such want, desire, suffer, hope, are happy, make plans and know that sooner or later they will die? Now, it is a fact that people and the institutions that represent them act 'as if' generations will exist. That is how it always has been and presumably always will be. Ultimately, however, it is for all intents and purposes an assumption, one that is by and large shared by all. That is, we are all reasonably certain that future generations will exist because since time immemorial they have always come into existence and will therefore continue to do so, unless some accident should bring the history of the world to a sudden end.

From a metaphysical point of view, the absent agent we are dealing with, and which is fundamentally assumed in certain types of transgenerational actions, is a fictional entity, namely an entity that does not have spatial-temporal existence. In effect, it is an entity lacking any traditional form of existence – it is instead the result of our imagination. Once it comes into being, however, that entity cannot but affect reality in its turn. In other words, the idea is that future generations have something in common with entities such as Cervantes's Don Quixote or Tolstoy's Count Bezúkhov – entities that exist nowhere except in the minds of their authors, in the books that contain their tales and in the minds of their readers. They are entities that writers imagine for the purpose of telling their stories, creating fictional characters that populate fictional worlds.[11]

Annie Thomasson in *Fiction and Metaphysics* introduces the concept of 'abstract artefact'[12] to explain fictional entities. From an ontological point of view at least, future generations are something similar to fictional entities. Given that as social agents we need to introduce a second agent, somebody other than the agent who initiates the transgenerational action, to bring to term the process of the transgenerational social action, thus we introduce in our world census a new entity, namely future generations. As such, the concept of abstract artefact appears a good candidate to help us explain future generations.

(Abstract) Artefacts

An artefact is an object created by somebody as a precise intentional act and for a purpose, from which it follows that artefacts are normally constructed to fulfil a specific function. Intentionality and purpose thus allow us to effectively distinguish various types of objects, such as, for example, a table – an object intentionally designed to meet a purpose – and a mountain – an object that instead does not depend on either a purpose or an intention. The mountain is simply there where we see it; it is totally mind-independent, and to comprehend it we need to study a great many things that in no way depend on us, such as the material of which it is made, how it is shaped, when it was formed and how it has changed. All those observations will serve to support, or otherwise invalidate, the theories of those who study mountains.

As a result, we classify mountains in the realm of natural things, but we intuitively grasp that tables are something different. Mountains, for instance, do not serve a purpose – they do not exist to block the wind or to give us snow. We are the ones who have learned to utilize them to satisfy our own needs, for instance, to go skiing when we like or to climb them every now and then. Tables, on the contrary, are designed so that human beings can rest objects on them. They essentially serve that purpose, in that they fulfil the function of bearing objects, and the ways they are designed serve to best fulfil that function. The extent to which a table more or less effectively fulfils the function for which it is made leads us to conclude whether it is a good table or not. Of course, in the general scheme of tables there can be variants – draughtsmen work on inclined planes, for instance – but they are not random developments, but rather variants introduced to meet a specific purpose, and hence imbued with a specific function.

The process of producing artefacts is determined by mind-dependence, which is especially important in the creation of prototypes. Consider the case of a craftsman who has the intention of creating a prototype of an artefact that has never been produced before. The artefact will be an object of his own invention. To create it, the craftsman will need to develop a certain idea in his mind of the object to be created and have the technical skills to transform the idea into a thing, as well as the capability of making it or, alternatively, he may engage somebody else to make it for him. Given that our craftsman is creating something completely new, he will have no script to follow or draw from. As such, he will need to develop an original idea and detail it in the process of its making, where the idea will have to encompass the main characteristics of the object in terms of its physical and functional properties, as well as the instructions for how it is to be made.

Let us suppose that our craftsman has constructed x and that x is a completely novel object, one that had never before been conceived or constructed, and that x has been successfully created. At that point, the craftsman will presumably have ideated at least two distinct things: (1) a new object and (2) a certain process fit to make it. The latter will allow him, finally, to standardize the process, rendering it endlessly repeatable. Those who repeat the process, that is, those wishing to remake x, naturally will be weakly bound to what our original craftsman first thought and made. The bond will be weak because the craftsmen who work on what the original craftsman created may introduce any number of variations without affecting the identity of x in practice. Such variants may concern either the physical characteristics of the object or the procedures for its making.[13] Those who make x after having acquired the idea from the original craftsman and having learned from him the technical procedure for making it will be able to make an 'x' that is similar but not identical to the prototype by following similar but not identical procedures.

A number of things can be derived from all this. First, that the original craftsman along with all the others that come after him will have an epistemic privilege regarding x. That is evident to the extent that they are the cause of x – first they imagine it, then they develop the idea in detail and finally they make it. Time and the manifold productions of x will then determine changes in some of its characteristics, though in general they will not alter its substance. Second, the original craftsman, just like all the others, in one way or another, needs to have a precise idea of the object he is creating. Of course, the original craftsman of the artefact will have developed an idea or a series of ideas that depend more or less entirely on him and on the functions the artefact is to fulfil. The craftsmen that come after him will instead have his idea as their reference point, to which they will add the modifications that have proved significant in offering new functions to the artefact, and which have been made by those who have altered the functionality of the object by pursuing promising paths from a functional point of view. That said, it is crucial to remember two things: first, the clear dependency of artefacts on their creators; and second, the epistemic privilege that the creators enjoy with respect to the artefacts they have created.

In contrast to concrete artefacts such as chairs, tables, motor vehicles and computers, the abstract artefacts of which Thomasson speaks do not occupy space-time in any traditional way, despite being designed and constructed by humans. With concrete artefacts they share the characteristic of being the product of human intentionality, unlike other human products, such as waste.[14] Thus, it would appear that intentionality, along with mind-dependence, are characteristics belonging to artefactuality.

On a closer look, it can also be noted how some objects – things that we would easily agree to class as artefacts – reveal how their artefactuality is compatible with a sort of spontaneous emergence of artefactual elements, thereby limiting to some extent the weight of intentionality. Thomasson gives as examples paths and villages. Let us take villages. It is plausible to think of villages as the outcome in part of an intentional design process and in part of a rather disorderly process lacking any precise design, which together determine the development of an urban centre.[15] Alternatively, and in all likelihood quite frequently, it can also be the case that a certain number of houses, arisen by chance in a certain place, come to be considered a village at a certain point by institutional stipulation. In that case, while it is true that no intentional activity can be considered the cause of the formation of the village, it is also true that we can identify intentional activity in the act of considering a certain number of houses located in a certain place as something more than a mere aggregate, or as a village.

Thus, even in circumstances in which a preliminary form of intentionality would appear to be rather weak, or entirely lacking, an artefact can still emerge, as the process is made possible by precise structures or configurations of reality – in this case, for instance, it can occur because the houses making up the aggregate of a 'village' are located within a few kilometres of each other. The fact that there can be a village where what we find is an aggregate of houses means that the existence of the village depends continuously on the existence of the houses. So if a terrorist group, for instance, were to blow up the near totality of those buildings, the village could go back to being classified as a mere aggregate of houses.

Artefacts, therefore, refer back to an idea of functionality and imply an act of design – all things that are tied in some way to intentionality. Yet, it still does not suffice because thinking about artefacts also means placing the focus on dependency relationships. Whenever we say that *if a exists, then b necessarily exists*, without specifying the time, we are talking about dependency, which simply means that at any unspecified time, where this type of dependency holds, if there is an *a*, then there must be a *b* too. Put that way, the dependency is very general, but it can be circumscribed to two forms of dependency. Here, we will talk about constant dependency, the first form, when the relationship between two entities is such that one entity requires the presence of the other to exist. However, we will talk about historical dependency, the second form, when the relationship is such that for a certain entity, let us say a, to come into being, another entity, let us say b, is necessary. An example of constant dependency is given by the relationship between the mind and the brain – for the mind to exist, the brain must exist constantly. The example is quite evidently one of rigid dependency, where if the existence of the mind depends on the existence of the brain, it follows that the brain belongs to the mind and is therefore an essential part of it. Constant dependency can be witnessed not only between objects but also between the states of things. To be a European citizen, for instance, there has to exist an institution called Europe, for which European citizens will exist so long as Europe exists.

However, it can also be that for an entity to exist, it requires the existence of another entity at the moment of its creation, without that implying the need for that dependency to continue in the future. This form of dependency, as we said, is called historical dependency. The existence of each and every human being depends on their parents. From a metaphysical perspective, that dependency does not cease to be binding once we are born. Oedipus, king of Thebes, depends on Jocasta and Laius not only as their son but also as king of Thebes.

Issues tied to dependency relationships are especially useful for understanding artefacts, in particular the abstract artefacts constituted by fictional entities. Such entities are often associated with a specific cultural or symbolic importance and value, as is clearly the case with the laws of a state or the characters of a novel. Where a writer intentionally outlines the boundaries of a fictional world and fills in the details, we will have that world and its details in exactly the same way that a lawmaker who follows the proper procedures for making laws will offer us new laws. There are certain techniques that are necessary for writing a novel, however good or bad it may be, just as there are certain techniques that are necessary for drafting a law. That is what gives rise to the artefactual nature of those objects, even though, in contrast with the majority of everyday artefacts, they are not concrete objects. As objects, they are unlike natural objects because they show a certain mind-dependence, in the sense that they would not be possible without humans conceiving or creating them. Such dependency, however, does not invalidate their reality nor their endurance over time, as their existence cannot be denied when it suits us.

Furthermore, unlike the majority of artefacts that exist in space and time, abstract artefacts often appear to exist in different ways and to show a certain vagueness in character, for which they generally cannot be defined in very detailed ways. It should be stressed how such vagueness follows from the nature of the object itself. Chairs need to satisfy set configurations to meet the purposes for which they were conceived; a novel or a law, on the other hand, can be broadly interpreted, and those interpretations all contribute to the identity of the object. For example, let us take this extract from *War and Peace*,

> One of the next arrivals was a stout, heavily built young man with close-cropped hair, spectacles, the light-colored breeches fashionable at that time, a very high ruffle, and a brown dress coat. This stout young man was an illegitimate son of Count Bezúkhov, a well-known grandee of Catherine's time who now lay dying in Moscow. The young man had not yet entered either the military or civil service, as he had only just returned from abroad where he had been educated, and this was his first appearance in society. Anna Pávlovna greeted him with the nod she accorded to the lowest hierarchy in her drawing room. But in spite of this lowest-grade greeting, a

look of anxiety and fear, as at the sight of something too large and unsuited to the place, came over her face when she saw Pierre enter. Though he was certainly rather bigger than the other men in the room, her anxiety could only have reference to the clever though shy, but observant and natural, expression which distinguished him from everyone else in that drawing room. [...] Pierre murmured something unintelligible, and continued to look round as if in search of something. On his way to the aunt he bowed to the little princess with a pleased smile, as to an intimate acquaintance. Anna Pávlovna's alarm was justified, for Pierre turned away from the aunt without waiting to hear her speech about Her Majesty's health. [...] But Pierre now committed a reverse act of impoliteness. First he had left a lady before she had finished speaking to him, and now he continued to speak to another who wished to get away. With his head bent, and his big feet spread apart, he began explaining his reasons for thinking the abbé's plan chimerical.[16]

Pierre is a tall, massive man who wears glasses; he is intelligent, but uncouth, and slightly awkward in his movements. It is an awkwardness of temperament that reveals itself in his manners, as notes Anna Pávlovna, a lady accustomed to inferring the character of her guests by closely observing how they comport themselves in society life. Tolstoy reveals much of the young count's temperament in this early description of the character, and much more of his personality will emerge as the novel wears on. He sews a sort of suit around Bezúkhov that reveals his main character traits, but without listing them all, in part because fictional characters are never saturate, or at least they can never be as saturate as a chair, for instance, whose physical characteristics also present the barriers to its use, and in part because the fictional worlds to which fictional characters belong require the interpretation of their readers to be completed. Every interpretation completes and enriches the object.

Streams of words have been devoted to the character of the young count and his view of the world. The vagueness or, rather, a certain vagueness of his character and of the possibilities that would be consistent with his character is a necessary condition for Bezúkhov to be the character that he is and for him to capture the interest of the readers of *War and Peace*. The chair artefact, on the other hand, does not permit the same level of vagueness, as otherwise it would be impossible to make use of the artefact for the purposes for which it was designed and made. Abstract artefacts are therefore something different to concrete artefacts. As artefacts, they need to be observed as objects that depend on their creators. In relation to their creators, they show a historical dependency; in relation to their novels, they show a constant dependency. As entities, however, they cannot be located precisely in space-time – it would be rather naive to claim that Count Bezúkhov shares the same spatial and temporal existence as a paperback copy of *War and Peace*.

All this gives us good grounds, I believe, to argue that future generations are entities similar to fictional characters, and hence abstract artefacts. The analogies are fairly self-evident, at a certain level of analysis at least. Just like Count Bezúkhov, the concept of future generations is a created concept that depends on those who created it. Intuitively, that means those who belonged to previous generations. It is clear how future generations are tied to previous generations by a relationship of historical dependency – without them, they would not be. Further on I will explain in what terms that is true and within which limits. Moreover, it would appear reasonable to argue that future generations also show a constant dependency on the social, institutional and historical context. Even here, such dependency is interesting and in certain ways complex, but I will return to that.

Behind all this, there is an important point that should be noted, a point which is similarly of an ontological nature: while fictional entities are and always will be abstract entities, as they do not and never will exist in space-time, sooner or later future generations – barring unpredictable and certainly undesirable catastrophes – will exist. In other words, as the name itself suggests, future generations are an entity that envisages a passage of status from being potential to being actual. Thus, they are destined to become present generations, which changes things quite considerably.

What kind of thing is a future generation?

Having seen the similarities, it is important now to focus on the dissimilarities. Major differences exist between fictional characters and future generations, such that to treat future generations as abstract artefacts, first we need to introduce significant changes to our model.

The first difference is macroscopic, one that we have already touched on. Count Bezúkhov is a fictional character, which means that he will always be just that – his form of existence will forever be restricted to the fictional world outlined in the pages of *War and Peace*. Future generations are instead characterized by a hybrid form of being. Initially they are conceived as abstract artefacts, showing a historical dependency on those who first ideated the concept, but that dependency is less definite than the dependency that ties a fictional character to its author. With the exception of certain problematic cases, the author of a novel is generally known, for which the historical dependency of a character is something that can be established rather easily.

However, even fictional characters can present problematic cases. The Homeric Question is a good example. Scholars now largely agree that the *Iliad* and *Odyssey* came to have the form in which we know them towards the start of the so-called Greek Dark Age (straddling the eighth and seventh centuries BCE, with the *Iliad* standardized before the *Odyssey*), thanks to the work of two brilliant poets, who drew on the cantos produced by the long oral tradition of *aodoi* and *rhapsodes*. We also know that there is no real certainty as to the historical identity of Homer, for which the lack of reliable historical sources, paired with the structure of the poems, has led scholars to conclude that Homer, as related to us, probably never existed at all. If that is true, then the historical dependency of the *Iliad* and *Odyssey* on the figure of Homer is something imaginary, given that the dependency is entirely fictional. Instead, what we do know is that behind the *Iliad* and *Odyssey* there was a plurality of authors, of whom we know next to nothing.

The case of future generations can arguably be understood analogously. Strictly speaking, at least two things are not clear about future generations, namely, who the authors were of the concept of a certain generation, x, and which generations effectively conditioned generation x. We know for sure that the concept of a certain generation – the specific abstract artefact we have identified as x – depends on the generation that preceded it, but identifying the terms of that dependency is generally rather complicated, as elements such as distance in time, the identity of its members and the dynamics of transgenerational relationships are all difficult to determine with any precision.

As such, only two points can be asserted with certainty. First, we know that a historical dependency exists between a future generation and past generations, and that the dependency is vague, in the sense it is not entirely clear which and how many generations contributed to the formation of the concept of a specific future generation. On the other hand, if it is simply a matter of defining which generation a certain generation depends on, then the historical dependency we are dealing with is determined. Moreover, and this is the second point, we know that the dependency tying generation x to previous generations is a constant dependency. That dependency is both strict, in that without past generations, future generations cannot exist, and vague, as identifying exactly which generation a certain future generation depends on is not all that straightforward. Therefore, while it is clear that no future generation can exist unless another generation existed before it, conceived the concept of it and outlined its conditions of possibility, the vagueness of the historical dependency that appears to constituently characterize the relationship between the generations appears to complicate things, at least from a metaphysical point of view.

In this framework, we can plausibly say that the historical dependency tying two generations concerns at least two aspects – the biological aspect of family descendance, on the one hand, and the matter of the ideation and use of the concept of future generation, on the other. As we have seen, biological descendance is a necessary condition for the direct passage of generations, representing the dimension that obviously concerns the passage of generations over time. But while a temporal dependency on who comes before is a necessary requirement for the passage of generations over time to be possible, no such necessity exists for spatial relationships of dependency.

Let us take the example of a boy born in Africa to African parents, who has come to Europe for his education. He will have peers of the same age in Africa as well as in Europe, and so he will belong equally to a generation in Africa and to a generation in Europe, even though his specific biological transgenerationality ties him to Africa. Thus, space does not determine an unequivocal, direct dependency, but only ties us culturally – this African native will belong to African culture and will only feel European after effectively coming into contact with cultural customs and usages, which initially will seem strange to him. Generational membership is therefore certainly determined by collocation in time as well as by location in space, where the latter comes to prominence especially when it is related to cultural elements characterizing a certain area of space. That means that a certain space becomes significant above all for the cultural determinations associated with it.

To review. I have argued that future generations are an abstract artefact that shows a strict, yet vague historical dependence on its authors. I have also argued that, unlike most abstract artefacts, this particular artefact at a certain point changes state to become a concrete collective entity – an entity determined by men and women who exist in a certain space and for a certain time. That is, while Don Quixote will never exist, future generations at a certain point will become present generations. That change of state is implicit in the concept of future generations, and it is what renders the concept not only interesting from an ontological point of view but above all useful from the perspective of social dynamics. In other words, it is precisely because future generations will exist that it makes sense to introduce the artefact into the social world and to interpret it according to meanings and practices that can go in a conservative or, alternatively, a regulatory direction.

Just as in the case of Frankenstein or Count Bezúkhov, therefore, the artefact 'future generation' is identified by a series of properties, which are what make it what it is. Those properties, however, can change depending on whether we choose to treat future generations as an artefact with a regulatory function or with a conservative function. If it is true that Kant saw in the concept of future generations an ethical and regulatory function setting the ideal towards which a society should strive to promote its self-preservation, it is just as true that over time, the conservative and normative acceptation of the concept has prevailed.

Hume was one of the first philosophers to have shown an awareness of the question:

> But the contract, on which government is founded, is said to be the original contract; and consequently may be supposed too old to fall under the knowledge of the present generation. If the agreement, by which savage men first associated and conjoined their force, be here meant, this is acknowledged to be real; but being so ancient, and being obliterated by a thousand changes of government and princes, it cannot now be supposed to retain any authority. If we would say any thing to the purpose, we must assert that every particular government which is lawful, and which imposes any duty of allegiance on the subject, was, at first, founded on consent and a voluntary compact. But, besides that this supposes the consent of the fathers to bind the children, even to the most remote generations […],

besides this, I say, it is not justified by history or experience in any age or country of the world.[17]

Hume describes transgenerationality in a peculiarly political key, where consent generates agreement, and it is that agreement that binds subjects to respect the social contract. That bond should be binding on those who decided to accept it, yet it is obvious in a way that it also binds their children and their children's children. Yet, as Hume perceptively notes, it is a stretching of affairs that has no foundation in fact. It is not appropriate to think it possible to bind the wills of those who have not voluntarily entered into the social contract, which perhaps, is the first vulnerability of every political system.

Then there is another vulnerability, one that we have already mentioned in passing, which is similarly tied to transgenerationality and typical of democracies. Democratic governments, more than others, are faced with the tricky problem of maintaining and managing their approval. Without approval, power changes hands. Given that policies that pay heed to transgenerational concerns are necessarily long term in vision and medium or long term in the programmes they underpin, it is clear that democratic systems – unless made up of citizens extremely sensitive to the higher and more sophisticated and complex dimensions of humankind – will always find themselves, from this point of view, in trouble.

As such, Hume was of the view that it is not legitimate to consider future generations as a mere means to the end of organizing power and maintaining popular approval, for which the conservative use that politicians tend to make of the concept of future generations is similarly not legitimate. In that case, future generations, when they are still future generations, should not be invoked in the management and consolidation of a certain political situation or as a guarantor of the welfare of a certain generation.

Thus, it is one thing to consider future generations as a regulatory ideal, along the lines of the Kantian model, where the concept enables future society to be harmonized and planned on the basis of the sphere of possibilities afforded by present society; but it is another to use the concept to fix the present or, worse, to pursue projects that would not be possible without mortgaging the future as a pledge to secure the benefits that can come in the present, and thus be enjoyed by present generations. The latter case clearly raises problems of justice, as in practice future generations are not treated as an end unto themselves, but rather as a means by which a certain society, in a certain moment, guarantees itself the possibility of accomplishing certain objectives, whatever they may be.

To put it another way again, while future generations could be the regulatory principle permitting us to plan and shape the future, more often than not they become the means we use to expand the present's capacity to make an impact by broadening its sphere of influence and opening up possibilities that otherwise would not be at hand. The point, however, is that not all that is possible is also due to us. So, as often as it may be that reference is made to future generations as a useful fiction allowing a certain world view to be prolonged (the world view of those introducing the concept) and a certain range of needs to be fulfilled, the choice to do so is in fact illegitimate, for two reasons. First, it binds in a very strict way the will and options open to future generations, more often than not without checking, even ex-post, their agreement; and second, it does all this without taking into consideration their interests – a circumstance that is all the more aggravating.

As illegitimate as it is, the conservative vision appears naturally to end up becoming by far the most prevalent acceptation of the concept in democratic systems, where it is imagined, from a completely functional perspective, that future generations will simply accept and bring to term our world plan and idea of humankind. That plan and idea is a sort of metaphysical extension of our collective identity and of the decisions taken by that identity through the organisms delegated to represent it. Thus, the concept of future generations is, all things considered, a rather vague artefact, lacking in detail, but its vagueness is functional, serving the purpose for which the abstract artefact was created, which more often than not is the conservative and more immediate, or easier acceptation of the concept – one which is often not without a predatory end.

In general, all those who make use of future generations to govern certain social dynamics suppose that future generations will behave exactly the way we behave, on the assumption that they will largely accept our values and share our criteria of justice. In short, they take for granted the idea that they will follow a line of conduct substantially similar to our own. It is truly astonishing to observe how people and institutions generally never call into doubt the endurance in time or the legitimacy of this mechanism. Take, for example, young Americans deciding not to pay the public debt contracted by their parents and their parents' parents. Think of what would happen on Wall

Street and at ranking agencies and investment banks if just the whiff of such a doubt should arise. Nothing is plainer than the fact that a generation will fulfil the obligations undertaken by the generation that preceded it. It is of no concern to us to know the details of the preferences, taste, religious beliefs or sexual orientations of the people belonging to a certain generation; suffice it to know or presume that future generations will do what we expect them to do. That is why in the social systems we construct, made of compacts, promises and subtle mechanisms to preserve, strengthen or weaken trust, we put into place such strict limits to ensure that transgenerational actions are brought to term. Otherwise, the costs in terms of undermined social trust would be extremely high.

Unlike in the case of Pierre Bezúkhov, whose identity is determined by the physical and moral characteristics that Tolstoy attributed to the character and by the overall narrative structure of which he is a part,[18] the abstract artefact 'future generations' can be attributed on the whole to two orders of properties. The first order, what I have called the 'conservative' acceptation, treats future generations as a sort of guarantor permitting other generations to do what they like, how they like. The second order, what I have called the 'regulatory' acceptation, sees future generations as functioning effectively as a regulatory principle for the construction and development of a society built to last. We have highlighted how the conservative scenario takes for granted, and therefore neglects, the willingness of future generations to take up the duty between generations, where it is precisely the assumption of such willingness that guarantees its reliability. Reliability generates trust, and trust enables the social mechanism to last through the long term.

Thus, in the conservative scenario, future generations are reliable by definition and by necessity. They are, after all, fictional entities, and so just as Tolstoy chose to give Pierre Bezúkhov an introspective disposition, Manzoni to make Don Abbondio a coward, Cervantes to give Don Quixote a lucid madness, and Ferrante to bestow a special maliciousness to Lulu, politicians similarly choose to consider future generations as a sort of projection of the people they govern, thereby creating a new entity that in many ways is continuous with the world they already know. Ultimately, however, there is no real reason for that effectively to be the case.

It is fair to ask whether such conclusions are justified. It is unlikely that human history will come to an end shortly, for which it is entirely probable that future generations will exist. That said, there is an inference that remains to be justified. From the fact that future generations are possible, it does not follow that they will be reliable, in the sense that they will behave or will be required to behave as we expect them to. It could be argued, in support of the conservative approach, that human behaviour is largely reiterative in character, and, indeed, we do tend to repeat known behaviours and patterns of behaviour. Yet there is no good reason to believe that such a state of affairs will continue indefinitely, going against all common sense and all ethical principles.

It is something workers in Italy know well, if somewhat confusedly, especially those who are now paying the price of the disastrous decisions made by the Rumor government.[19] It was that government which took the decision of giving women with children and public-sector workers the option of retiring at the age of forty years on an old-age pension. The policy proved disastrous for the public purse and profoundly unfair in terms of the cost to be borne and the inequality of treatment afforded to citizens born at different times, as those who were able to benefit from the 'Rumor treatment' were privileged with respect to the rest of the workforce, which was left burdened with the cost and forced to retire on very different, substantially much less favourable conditions.

The exact terms of the matter will be addressed further on, but for now the point is that people in the workforce today will have to work much longer than the people who benefited from that law, and their pensions will be considerably lower. So it is no surprise if they call for a review of the transgenerational bond that binds them morally and materially to bear the onerous costs of those pensions. Yet, if governments agreed to review the obligation, the consequences in turn would be morally and ethically highly questionable – imagine a society that cuts or even cancels the pensions of men and women who today are aged between eighty and ninety years. Such a decision would be cruel, made to the detriment of people no longer able to change their way of life, and so ultimately the decision would not be acceptable.

Nevertheless, the fact remains that the compact made by the state, forged by the Rumor government and the citizens who voted for that parliamentary majority, was a depraved and unfair compact, one that brought the government benefits in the form of votes, as Italian citizens confirmed their willingness to benefit from it, thumbing their nose at all the possible consequences. With all that, future generations were left with the greater part of the bill to pay, violating in all senses the transgenerational bond. That government perpetrated the perfect crime, encouraged by the democratic dynamics of winning and maintaining power – dynamics that, as we know all too well, bring consistent benefits to the voters of a certain system and to them alone, without institutions generally troubling themselves with finding corrective measures from a transgenerational point of view. Italy still today carries the scars, in terms of the economic and social costs, of that and other similar decisions. It was a compact that was clearly illegitimate and should never have been made, as it prejudiced the rights of one of the parties to it. Such a premiss, however, still does not provide the grounds to conclude that those who find themselves forced to honour it are justified in disaffirming it, as the predictable consequences of breaking the compact would be just as unacceptable. Hence future generations have been compelled to uphold the transgenerational bond, proving their reliability as the generations that preceded them hoped they would.

Let us now turn to the second point, which is the mixed form of potential and actual being that identifies future generations. The observations so far lead to the conclusion that there is at least one major difference between a fictional entity (such as Don Quixote) and future generations. The former, or fictional character, will never come alive, as it is identified by a form of existence that is both made possible and circumscribed by fictional space. If a killer parasite were to attack and destroy every single copy of *Don Quixote* and wipe out the memory of every single person who has read it and remembers it, in that case we could say that Don Quixote simply would not exist anymore and probably would never exist again, given that the character's existence is limited to and depends on the medium containing it, even if only the imperfect memory of Cervantes' readers.

On the other hand, future generations in all likelihood will exist in space and time, or more precisely they will exist in a space that will largely coincide with what was our own but in a time that is not our own. In other words, barring the unpredictability of events, future generations will move from being possible to being actual because, in their case, possibility is destined to give way to actuality, which means individuals in flesh and blood, who desire, suffer, rejoice, who live and breathe. The consideration obliges us to review our metaphysical analysis, at least in part. Just as fictional characters are fictional objects, so the concept of future generations is a fictional concept – they do not exist outside the minds of those who conceive of them. Unlike fictional objects, however, future generations have a form of existence that is destined to move from the possible to the actual, or from potential being to being. Thus, we are dealing with abstract artefacts that will become concrete groups, namely generations that live in a certain time period and in a certain space. The metaphysically interesting point is that the concrete group (the future generation that occupies certain space-time coordinates) shows a dependency on the abstract artefact that is both historical and genetic, such that the abstract artefact determines the characteristics and possibilities of the concrete group.

Thus, we have a first reply to the common-sense argument expressed by Woody Allen's quip, 'Why should we put ourselves out of our way for future generations; what have they ever done for us?' The answer is simple. As abstract artefacts characterized by a form of existence that changes from being possible to actual, they have made a major part of our social life possible. That is true even in the countless circumstances in which a conservative acceptation is adopted of the concept of future generations.

Actions

Let us recapitulate what I have said so far, before moving on with the inquiry into the particular type of social actions that we call transgenerational actions.

To begin with, I defended the argument that transgenerationality is primitive, and as such it forms our identity as social individuals. As social and political animals, human beings are naturally inclined to building relationships, many of which are medium or long term. In most cases, those relationships involve individuals who are not bound by blood or family ties; thus, they are weak relationships.

The transgenerational bond, just like any other bond, is first and foremost an obligation, implying both rights and duties. There exist two types of transgenerational bonds. The first is the bond that exists between the various generations of the one family unit, a bond that is broadly contemplated in the architecture of social reality and hence protected from a normative point of view. The fact that the generational passage from parent to child is typically identified, among other things, by the transfer of the family name by patriarchal line, or sometimes by matriarchal line, or more rarely by both, suggests how the use of a family name is considered an external and distinctive sign indicating that in the passage from parent to child 'something' is preserved. In its minimal form, that 'something' is biological heritage. In situations of this kind, which are the simplest to identify and define, it is held that what is transmitted is the biological and, hence, constituent structure of living beings. Such transmission is permitted by an important affective tie. Consider the case in which x is the mother or father of y, who is therefore the son or daughter of x. Here, biological inheritance will consist of the passage of part of the being of x (that part, at least, tied to his/her biological heritage) to y, for which x will feel a particular bond with y, in the sense of a natural continuity. The biological transgenerational bond is characterized by the fact that generational passage is first of all understood as the transmission of something physical, and hence something clearly identifiable and definable. All this gives rise to the idea that the transmission of genetic heritage in a certain way implies that the material goods belonging to the parent should similarly be 'transmitted', for which the parental relationship implies not only the transfer of biological heritage but also the transfer of material goods.

Now, this kind of transgenerationality, or what we have called primary or basic transgenerationality, is generally recognized in all cultures and is formally protected by law. It is interesting, for instance, to observe how certain legal systems, such as Italy's, contemplate strict rules concerning the inheritance by children of the parents' estate, regardless of the will of the parents, for which if a parent wishes to exclude a child from the inheritance, 'forced estate' provisions will be activated to guarantee the interests of basic transgenerationality. There is, generally, a common-sense idea, therefore, that the continuity between x and y is an objective element that should be protected, even from a legal standpoint, regardless of the intentions of the bearers of the transgenerational relationship. The means available to legal systems to give shape to such protection range from the recognition of paternity – very strict requirements generally have to be met for paternity to be denied – to the protection of the child in terms of material support. Basic transgenerationality is therefore a clearly identifiable bond, which is similarly clearly protectable and protected. Thus, it essentially appears as a state, a way of being.

Alongside primary transgenerationality, we then identified another type of transgenerationality, which we called secondary transgenerationality. I believe that secondary transgenerationality is a condition of possibility for the existence of social reality, such that without secondary transgenerationality, social reality would simply be impossible, at least not in the complex, structured forms that we know. We defined secondary transgenerationality as a transgenerational relationship that does not necessarily include, as a condition of possibility, a parental relationship or consanguinity, meaning that blood or family ties need not be envisaged for it to exist.

I then explained how Immanuel Kant, in his political philosophy, explored how the intergenerational relationship not only exists but also is characterized by a particular structure. In his *Idea for a Universal History with a Cosmopolitan Purpose*,[20] he argued that, as a first proposition, 'All the natural capacities of a creature are destined sooner or later to be developed completely and in conformity with their end'; and as a second proposition, 'In man (as the only rational creature on earth), those natural capacities which are directed towards the use of his reason are such that they could be fully developed only in the species, but not in the individual.'

In those two propositions, Kant stresses two points in particular. The first is that the natural capacities and faculties of living creatures are developed and reach their full potential only over time. Which is to say that time is necessary for human beings to fully develop their potentials and talents and become fully able to give shape and order to their energies. The second, in relation to human beings, is that all natural capacities that seek to use reason will find complete accomplishment not in the individual, but in humankind. By that, Kant's intention is to stress that relationships within the species are relationships that evidently are organized with particular effectiveness and in a complete way only over the course of time – specifically, over a very long time span. Thus, temporality allows reason to unfold fully in the life of individuals.

> Reason, in a creature, is a faculty which enables that creature to extend far beyond the limits of natural instinct the rules and intentions it follows in using its various powers, and the range of its projects is unbounded. But

reason does not itself work instinctively, for it requires trials, practice and instruction to enable it to progress gradually from one stage of insight to the next. Accordingly, every individual man would have to live for a vast length of time if he were to learn how to make complete use of all his natural capacities; or if nature has fixed only a short term for each man's life [...], then it will require a long, perhaps incalculable series of generations, each passing on its enlightenment to the next.[21]

Kant's underlying idea is that human nature is profoundly imperfect, a 'warped wood', as he remarks in the sixth proposition, which can never be straightened out. For human beings are governed by two opposing instincts, one that leads them to join and live in society, and another which leads them to isolate themselves and live as individuals. In practice, humans are torn between a tendency to cooperate and a tendency to impose their will in selfish and authoritarian ways. Nevertheless, Kant appears convinced that, not only does there exist a relationship between generations that serves a constituent function for social life, but also that such a relationship is of a positive and augmentative nature, in the sense of increasing tangible and intangible goods. So in practice, as imperfect and needy of guidance and direction as human nature is, the relationship between generations is intrinsically positive, bringing about a virtuous process in which each generation works in some way for the benefit of those that will follow.

> Yet nature does not seem to have been concerned with seeing that man should live agreeably, but with seeing that he should work his way onwards to make himself by his own conduct worthy of life and well-being. What remains disconcerting about all this is firstly, that the earlier generations seem to perform their laborious tasks only for the sake of the later ones, so as to prepare for them a further stage from which they can raise still higher the structure intended by nature; and secondly, that only later generations will in fact have the good fortune to inhabit the building on which a whole series of their forefathers (admittedly, without any conscious intention) had worked, without themselves being able to share in the happiness they were preparing.[22]

Putting aside the teleological perspective Kant takes, the underlying idea that each generation appears to act in the interests of later generations, or at least that each generation appears to be guided by a design that is not always discerned by observers, but which possesses an intrinsic unity of meaning, is interesting, as it suggests that the fruit of what a certain generation accomplishes can only be enjoyed fully and completely by the generations that follow. What is of interest here, however, is not so much the content of Kant's theory – Kant was ultimately an optimist, as it can easily be demonstrated that the transgenerational legacy is not always necessarily positive – but rather the fact that Kant considers secondary transgenerationality as self-evident.

Kant holds that secondary transgenerationality exists because nature exists, which to render human history something worthy, pursues a vast design. If that were not the case, humans would have remained warped pieces of wood. That is why transgenerationality, as Kant conceived of it in a fundamentally regulatory sense, exists regardless of the will of individuals. It is a part of a suprahistorical dimension in which human beings act and are made to act in spite of themselves, as it were, and without their knowledge of it. Therefore, Kant infers the existence of secondary transgenerationality from the dynamics of nature, where the fact that progress exists in human history depends on the objectives that nature sets – objectives that transcend individuals and are accomplished through the dynamics of secondary transgenerationality.

The question now is: given that Kant's teleological model can be disputed by potentially good reasons refuting it, is the concept of secondary transgenerationality similarly open to question? Or can we identify other arguments to those proposed by Kant to support it? Let us return to the matter of actions.

Basic actions and complex actions

The question of the definition of 'action' emerges essentially for two reasons. Besides the need to define what it is we call 'action', there is also the need to distinguish actions from simple occurrences, especially in cases where the properties of an action and an occurrence seem to be no different, that is, when they are apparently indiscernible. The question was posed by Ludwig Wittgenstein in relation to the logical status of actions. What remains if we subtract from the fact a person raises her arm, the fact that her arm rises? In other words, what distinguishes a simple occurrence, the arm rising, from an action, an agent raising her arm?

Causal theories are the most well known and the most debated of all action theories.[23] In general, they tend to circumscribe the explanation to the causes of the action, removing it from the matter of ontological constitution. Causal theories build on a key premise, namely what determines the distinction between action and occurrence does not lie in anything constituting the action itself, but rather in the causal chain that leads to the action. In other words, whatever it is we are investigating, when we are dealing with two indiscernible things, to distinguish them we have to look to the reasons that determine them and which caused them.

Thus, from the point of view of the ontology of action, what is crucially important is not so much to examine the structure of the action, but to reconstruct the genesis of the history of causes that determined a certain action. The approach is open to a precise objection raised, among others, by the US philosopher Harry G. Frankfurt,[24] which is that two identical actions can be determined by different causal chains, raising problems for the idea that the causal chain is a necessary and sufficient condition for identifying an action. For if we assume that the causes of an action are necessary and sufficient conditions for it, and accept, as we must necessarily, that different causes can lead to one and the same action, then we must also accept that it is not the causes that determine the identity of actions.

Hence, a different strategy to that proposed by causal theories needs to be identified. Frankfurt proposes that what decisively determines an action and allows it to be distinguished for all intents and purposes from a pure and simple movement is that intentional actions are determined by the will of the person performing them, who coordinates them as part of an overall scheme. For him, actions (including non-intentional actions) can always be ascribed to an organic plan. When that happens – think of all the different, yet coordinated actions performed by a pianist when playing a symphony, for instance – it is obviously impossible to think that they are merely simple movements. Now, it is self-evident that our bodies can perform both simple movements and actions without our noticing it or being aware of it in some way, as there are systems specifically purposed to control what Arthur Danto called 'basic actions'.[25] The important point, however, is that coordinated actions require a specific design, and that is what distinguishes a movement from true action.

Individual actions substantially fall within the sphere of a broader and more complex activity of design.

A taxonomy of collective actions

It is evident that not all actions are individual actions, in the sense of belonging to a single person. There are actions that are performed by at least two or more people, for which it is generally agreed that they exhibit a different structure to individual actions. An effective taxonomy of actions should therefore distinguish individual actions from collective actions, by isolating the identifying properties of collective actions.

The rather natural prerequisite for an action to be considered a collective action is that two or more agents act together, which roughly speaking means that they share an 'x', or the objective of the action. Now, the objective of the action can be shared in one of two different ways: (1) where two or more agents share the same objective on what might be called an accidental basis (e.g. a fire breaks out in a shopping mall and the people inside all behave in more or less the same way, with the implicit objective of saving themselves); or (2) where two or more agents can intentionally share one and the same objective (e.g. a fire breaks out and a team of fire fighters take action together to maximize their efforts to extinguish it).

Case (2) is of greater relevance for our purposes as it better instantiates collective action, so let us start there. The underlying question is, how is it possible for two or more people to act in such a way as to perform the most appropriate series of actions to fulfil an objective (such as to extinguish a fire)? The social ontologies that have addressed such questions for the most part introduce the notion of collective intentionality to underpin, in the intentions of their theorists and supporters,[26] the idea that there is a sort of biological predisposition for collective action. The strongest version of such a theory is probably that offered by John Searle, who theorizes collective intentionality as a primitive phenomenon that is prior to the disposition of human beings to perform individual actions.[27] Thus, for Searle, human beings are biologically disposed to acting collectively, by sharing intentional states such as believing, wanting and intending, from which it follows that individual intentionality is not sufficient to explain collective actions. Hence, Searle introduces the notion of collective intentionality as what makes collective actions possible. The players in a football match can only do what they do because they are biologically hard-wired for coordinated action – besides knowing how to act to play their roles, they are inclined and driven to cooperate, in the sense that they know how to execute a sort of intelligent collective action aimed at a purpose.

What is peculiar about Searle's theory is that collective intentionality can neither be reduced to individual intentionality nor described simply in terms of individual intentionality plus some extra property. Rather, he argues that collective intentionality is something radically distinct in nature. I shall call this the 'strong version' of the theory of collective intentionality.

Then there is a weak version of the theory put forth by the Finnish philosopher Raimo Tuomela.[28] For Tuomela, it is self-evident that in acting, human beings include other human beings in their action plans, which means that they anticipate them and, in part at least, their responses. Tuomela's position is fuller in its account and therefore captures certain aspects of reality better. For instance, he distinguishes three notions of collective intentionality on the basis of their specific relationship with objectives, as follows:

1. objectives that some people find they share accidentally;
2. objectives shared intentionally;
3. the objective of a collective.

Of these three types of collective actions, the weakest is obviously the first (1). It is the case, for example, of the people who all find themselves in the shopping mall when a fire breaks out. Predictably, they will all try to rush to the exit as quickly as possible. Therefore, everyone, in that situation, will share an objective not on the basis of a choice, but as a result of a state of affairs that causally determines the behaviour of the people involved. Besides sharing a specific objective (doing everything necessary to get to the exit as quickly as possible), the people affected by the fire will be aware of the objectives of the other unfortunate people involved. In other words, they will know that everyone, without exception, barring perhaps those with specific, contingent motives, will have the intention of rushing out as quickly as possible to save themselves. Therefore, to save themselves it will be important to organize their individual choices on the basis of those beliefs that correctly depend on the state of affairs.

The second type (2) of collective action calls for greater commitment. It implies that the people sharing a certain objective do so intentionally, but it also implies they have no common plan to achieved the shared objective. In the case of our shopping mall fire, people effectively react with surprise and probably panic in response to the sudden fire. Thus, they will share the objective of saving themselves, despite not having been able to share a plan to enable them to achieve the objective. Each person will want to save themselves, each will suppose that the others want the same, but there has been no time to devise a common plan. We might even suppose that, in such circumstances, they will each want to save themselves at the expense of the others.

The idea here is that the objective is shared, but the actions and action plans fit to achieve the objective are not (because the people could not or would not do so). In a situation of this kind, it is clear that the commitment towards the common objective is fairly weak – there is an intention, whether manifested by the agents or presumed, but there is no commitment undertaken by the agents as to how the intention will be achieved. That implies a significant margin of uncertainty over the possibility of the common objective realistically being achieved. But it is also reasonable, I believe, to raise a question mark over whether such a model of intentional collective action implies a commitment, as Tuomela suggests it does,[29] where a commitment concerning intentions implies collective intentionality, even where a single action is not put into place towards the objective. I will return later to this point.

Finally, the third type (3) of collective action described concerns actions that involve not only the identification of a shared objective but also of an action plan fit to achieve it. In this specific type of collective action, people cooperate to achieve an objective they have set jointly. It is evident that this group of collective actions can come about in very different ways. For instance, the objective may be shared by more or less numerous groups, by groups of people who belong to the group only by virtue of the objective, or by groups that share other, more important objectives and so on. What makes such actions a well-defined type is the fact that they entail agents voluntarily taking up a position, as well as the embodiment of that taking up of a position in a series of specific actions.

The framework Tuomela provides offers a series of prerequisites common to all collective actions. Specifically, (a) the fact that the people hold beliefs; and (b) in general, people who share numerous beliefs are led to choose the most advantageous option. For example, if finding myself in a fire, I decide to rush to the nearest exit as quickly as possible, I would expect: (i) that others in my same situation will hold beliefs concerning fires and how to save themselves; (ii) that those agents will plan actions and solutions similar to my own; and finally, (iii) that all those people will choose effectively to put into place the solutions they have devised.

Now, in the case of the people trapped in a shopping mall and threatened by flames, it is reasonable to believe that the majority will act according to predictable logics, at least as concerns the choice of objective of saving themselves. That conclusion will be valid as long as there are external constraints, whether practical or normative, on the agent that are rather strict and to some extent difficult to bypass. When that is not the case, or we find ourselves in cases (1) or (2), it often happens that the shared objectives will not be achieved.

In other words, in exploring collective or we-intentionality, the more interesting cases are those in which the world does not 'compel' the will of agents to cooperate through constraints of any sort, be they biological, normative or cultural. Transgenerational actions are just such a case. They are actions that typically are performed by P-institutions, that is, by people who act in the place of institutions, or by actual institutions or collective agents. As we have observed, such actions are characterized by being undertaken by one agent (with the authority to do so) and being brought to term by another agent (or agents) who is not the original agent. Agents who undertake a transgenerational action share an objective – or at least they do so under one possible description of the transgenerational action, while that may very well not be the case under other possible descriptions. Transgenerational actions are distinguished by their extension in time and are constituted by a complex of actions that, in accordance with the principle of ontological parsimony, can be reduced to a single description. Such a description is formulated on the basis of the common intention of the agents of the transgenerational action and explained on the basis of reasons. Therefore, the agents who undertake a transgenerational action are driven by the intention to do what they do because they share reasons that underlie the objective of the action. That is true in the case of conservative transgenerational actions, but in the case of regulatory transgenerational actions, the agents of the transgenerational action also share expectations that can be formulated on the basis of a certain transgenerational action. But where intentions can be justified on the basis of reasons, predictions can be justified on the basis of scientific evidence.[30]

Transgenerational actions

Transgenerational actions are defined, therefore, as a particular type of social action that transmits the transgenerational bond. As such, they are collective actions identified by certain properties that make them recognizable and distinguish them from other social actions, such as those performed by groups.

To identify their key characteristics, transgenerational actions are actions (a) performed by agents who undertake an action or a series of interconnected actions that (b) serve a common purpose and (c) are characterized by entailing and requiring a considerable extension in time. Furthermore, (d) transgenerational actions are *not* concluded by the agents who initiate them. Finally, (e) often they are actions that imply important consequences of a practical, ethical or economic nature. In substance, they are actions that necessarily must be taken into account due to both the central role they play in the organization of social reality and the long-term consequences they can generate.

So far so good, as concerns the structure of the action. However, another observation needs to be introduced, namely transgenerational actions generally have different types of impacts on the lives of the people who perform them. Or more precisely, the impacts they bear on the lives of the people who originate them are different to the impacts they have on the lives of those who bring them to term after a certain interval of time, *t*. And during that interval of time, the action can change certain elements of its structure.

Transgenerational actions rarely come 'at no cost'. Indeed, the fact that a significant and generally lengthy amount of time is required for a transgenerational action to be completed is typically tied to the 'cost' of the action. That cost can be measured in various ways, for instance, in relation to the time, common resources and energy needed for it. Transgenerational actions are, therefore, tied to the significant costs they incur in terms of needs, consumption of raw materials, consumption of common resources or the consumption of common social and economic wealth. In short, the cost-benefit ratio of a transgenerational action is a variable, for which an equilibrium repeatedly needs to be found between the use of the resources in question and the agents involved.

All this does not implicate, in principle, the nature of the impact of a transgenerational action, in the sense that it can be positive or negative – that is, its outcomes can be positive or perceived as positive by the people affected in various ways, or they can be negative or perceived as negative by the people affected in various ways. Thus, transgenerational actions are ethically neutral in and of themselves, but they can assume an ethical connotation depending generally on three factors, namely, the *intentions* of those who commit to them, the capacity of the transgenerational agents to produce accurate *predictions* as to their consequences and, finally, the *will* to put into practice appropriate decisions for the management of the transgenerational action and the most significant consequences tied to the action.

Such actions can also be performed by groups; however, it is important to stress a major difference with group actions. For if in group actions the objective is shared by the social agents belonging to the group, in the case of transgenerational actions the situation is different – a difference that marks a key point. In the case of transgenerational actions, the common objective is not necessarily shared by all the agents in some way involved in the action. It can easily be the case, for instance, that having imagined a transgenerational action *a*, the transgenerational agents who initiate action *a* at time *t* share a certain objective, which is the objective of the action, but the agents of action *a* at time t_1 may no longer share the original objective, but find themselves compelled to continue and bring to term the action initiated at time *t*.

Thus, it is evident how there can be a substantial asymmetry between the agents of a transgenerational action. Some, let us say a group, may share the main objectives of the action, in which case they will all be in a suitable position to identify the means to render the action effective and as consistent as possible with the objective set. Other agents of the same action, however, may find themselves bringing to term a transgenerational action whose means and ends they do not agree with. However, the fact that the latter group does not agree with the former on the objectives of the action cannot be a sufficient reason to abandon or reformulate the objectives.

Then there is a final point to be stressed concerning trust. It would appear that transgenerational actions effectively require a great deal of trust between the parties, for which it makes sense to explain exactly what it means to talk about trust in this context. Given that, in many cases, transgenerational actions do not appear to present objectives that are shared by the totality of the transgenerational agents involved, it is quite singular that people should trust in the possibility of a transgenerational action being brought to term as a foregone conclusion. In other words, why do we take it for granted that two generations should trust each other, or trust in what the other will do? Or more precisely, why does the earlier generation trust that the later generation will follow the path it has decided to lay out? From an even broader perspective, how can we justify the trust that the social system, in all its expressions, shows in things continuing to go in this way?

On a closer look, we can see how it is not at all easy to find a good answer to those questions because there does not appear to be any real reason why someone (a certain generation) should trust someone else, such as a different generation that will come to be rather far off in the future. So if trust implies knowledge, as we will see, then it would seem reasonable to ask, for instance, what kind of knowledge can one generation possess about another. Is it a kind of knowledge so profound and elaborate as to permit the establishment of a relationship of trust? If that were possible, would such a relationship of trust be justified and well grounded?

Let us start with the first point, to see if it is possible to circumscribe the horizon of meaning of the word 'trust'.

Trust

One point it is worth reflecting on concerns the implications of trust in relation to transgenerational actions. It is self-evident, in a way, that when we speak of actions that are protracted over time and that are performed by various agents who may not find themselves in the position of agreeing with the original objectives that motivated the action, the trust component plays a significant role. So let us now look at two questions: firstly, what is trust? And secondly, what sort of trust is present (or absent) in transgenerational actions?

Generally speaking, there is fairly wide support in the literature for the idea that trust is a type of relationship that, in certain conditions, gives a considerable advantage to the parties to the relationship. That advantage lies in the cognitive and emotional resources that are freed up and can be devoted and used for other purposes. Nevertheless, the advantage is only real to the extent to which the person who chooses to trust, and hence accepts to defer the advantage, thereby running the risk of potential loss or injury, has the means to choose in reasonably rational terms. Therefore, it is absolutely essential to have access to the relevant information before making any choice that implies an act of trust.

Now, keeping to this understanding of the concept of trust, it is clear how it is possible to speak of trust between people who know each other and, in many cases, know what they can expect from each other. But when it is a matter of trust between people and institutions, or even trust between institutions, the situation is more complicated. That is because a necessary condition for a relationship of trust, as I have outlined it here, to be established implies a certain cognitive transparency of the information that a certain x can have in relation to a certain y. It is easy to appreciate how difficult it is for a citizen who does not hold an eminent political office to have relevant information about the government of the country, for instance. In the best of scenarios, citizens may believe that such information is held by the politicians who represent them, whom they trust by virtue of having chosen them. Thus, the mechanism of political representation plays a delicate and central role, as it is through the choice of a specific representative that the relationship of trust, which is a necessary condition for the delegation of rights and the functioning of the political machine, is structured.

Therefore, good cognitive capacities and detailed information about the situation we are called to decide on constitute fundamental prerequisites for someone to come to trust another. That is true because every relationship of trust requires a rational premiss, or the awareness of choosing to run a risk in the future, which can be accepted on the basis of good reasons. If we accept such a notion of trust as a first approximation of the concept, then we can consider as standard a situation of the kind whereby x decides to trust y in relation to the pursuit of objective z on the grounds that, given all the information that x possesses about y, such information leads her to believe that y will act to protect the interests of x in relation to z. That is true because x knows that the interests of y fall within the scope of her own interests. In short, the reasons of y in relation to z are grounded on the reasons of x.

The relationship of trust is, therefore, a relationship built on two elements: the relationship between x and y, and the objective of that relationship, which we will call z. Hence it is generally a relationship circumstantiated by a specific objective, which means that where x trusts y, her trust in y does not extend to all aspects, but is limited to a determinate scope. Here we have a strong meaning of trust, but there is also a weaker meaning, which steers a great many of the decisions that appear to be taken within the scope of trust relationships, but which substantially depart from them.

We have said that trust depends on knowledge and have observed how, in many cases, there is no way to establish any real direct knowledge of what we ought or want to trust. Nevertheless, it happens all the same that we place our trust in people and institutions, for the most part because we manage to develop compensating relationships. For example, if it is undoubtedly true that as citizens we do not know all the dynamics characterizing the actions of government, that deficit is compensated by the relationships that parliamentarians hold with the electorates they represent. Such a state of affairs may lead us to believe that the parliamentarian will protect our interests in key matters, the consequence of which is that we will trust those we have elected.

Recapitulating, we can argue that the relationship of trust always implies two parties (whether people, institutions, governments or states), a string of knowledge circumstantiated by the objective that ties the two parties to the relationship and, finally, the awareness of running a calculated risk. Indeed, we know that the people or institutions with which we hold a relationship of trust in relation to matters that are sensitive or of some interest for our lives will make choices we agree with and that will bring some benefit even for us.

Placing our trust in someone or something is never a risk-free choice. The trust that x places in y will be embodied in an action that x does, and which will expose x to the risk of suffering some injury from y. Therefore, it is important to enter into a relationship of trust only if the risk is circumscribed, limited and in some way calculable. Given this context, it is natural to ask whether transgenerational actions, as we have outlined them, imply a relationship of trust. We have defined transgenerational actions as a type of action that endures for a considerable length of time. To be accomplished fully, an action of such a kind depends on various agents, belonging to various generations, taking up the burden of it. Therefore, transgenerational actions imply cooperation between various agents who, moreover, belong to different generations and generational contexts. Thus, they are actions that necessarily require agents to commit their wills in the future, as well as to trust that people who have not expressed any agreement to perform the action will commit themselves to bringing to term what was decided in the decision-making and implementing stages of the action. Hence it is not only those who initiate the transgenerational action who commit to binding their wills in the future but also those who follow them, as it will be up to them to push ahead with and complete the transgenerational action.

From that perspective, it would seem that some form of trust relationship must be implied. Nevertheless, the case warrants closer observation. In our specific case, the situation is not at all standard from at least two points of view. First, the architects of transgenerational actions are, in a great many cases, agents bearing different intentions, beliefs and volitions. Second, transgenerational actions – which, as we have extensively stressed, are per se neutral in structure and not ethically determined – can be connotated in a regulatory or a conservative sense. The conservative option deserves more special attention, as it concerns transgenerational actions that are conceived for the prevalent or exclusive advantage of those who decide to initiate the action, without first considering the matter of the longer-term consequences of the action.

Let us now turn to the first point, concerning the epistemological component of the relationship of trust. We necessarily have rather vague ideas when it comes to future generations. What can we really know about future generations? We can in part predict, and in part imagine, how they will or might be. As I have said, in long-term decision-making, a conservative and projective attitude generally prevails, for which it is easily tempting to use transgenerational actions in a conservative way, that is, to serve the needs of the present, while deferring the consequences to a different historical time and to different people. Such an option undoubtedly responds to short-term needs, which are often anything but noble, and assumes a corresponding idea of future generations as serving the purpose of completing transgenerational actions. In other words, the concept is functional for the accomplishment of a goal that, in many cases, serves to satisfy a specific need.

What we generally do here is move from the known to the unknown, from what we know about ourselves to depict how future generations might be, without showing any genuine interest in the future. We neglect to gather clues, to read social and economic data, and to make predictions, partly because it is all quite complex, partly because governments generally shun the utility of formulating predictions, preferring instead to use the future to satisfy present needs.

Turning back to the question of trust, it seems that only transgenerational actions of a regulatory nature imply any real relationship of trust. In such cases, the very structure of the transgenerational action, which retains traces of the attention focused on the collective interest, requires trust in the fact that those who in the future will become part of the transgenerational action will in turn uphold the regulatory nature of the action. As we have already discussed, any decision to grant trust implies a certain predictive capacity and, at the same time, a willingness to run a certain risk. Whenever we lend money to a friend, for instance, a predictive component comes into play as, on the basis of the information we have about our friend, his reliability, and ability to keep his word, we imagine that, sooner or later, he will pay back the amount we have lent him. Obviously, it is a predictive hypothesis formulated on the basis of the information we have about him, about his person and his personal history, which may either be confirmed, if he keeps his word and honours the debt, or disconfirmed, leaving us short of money, friendship and trust.

When we imagine future generations and the choices they will make or should make, the predictive component is certainly more marked – much more so than when reasoning about our friend and the debt that he owes us – for in the case of future generations, we have fewer circumstantiated details and less precise information on how they will be and the choices they will make. Nevertheless, we do have clues on which to build an idea of them, as the present already says a lot about how the future will be, and it is the means we have to try and steer the future.

We already know that transgenerational actions are often conservative in nature. When dealing with transgenerational actions of this kind, we are dealing with actions that primarily or exclusively aim to protect the well-being of the generations that originate them. In such cases, it is evident that the situation is not one of a certain generation protecting the interests of another generation. The same can generally be said of transgenerational actions that have to do with commons. Hence, when transgenerational actions are conservative in nature, it is obvious that the relationship of trust is not a practicable option, neither for the transgenerational agents who initiate the action nor for those who will step into their place to continue the action and ultimately bring it to term. Rather, the situation is one in which one generation imposes its own interests on another, without providing any good reasons why the later generation should bring to term the transgenerational action initiated by the earlier generation. When that happens, it is useful to have a normative apparatus in place to fill the gap left by the relationship of trust which cannot be established.

As a first approximation, therefore, we can assert that the two types of transgenerational action have different conditions of possibility. Conservative transgenerational actions demand a legal and political normativity that enables their full implementation, whereas regulatory transgenerational actions can be underpinned by a relationship of trust between the generations, based on a certain predictiveness, that is, a certain picture of the future outlined from an analysis of the facts and information offered by the present. Normativity obviously enables the consolidation and strengthening of what the relationship of trust permits us to develop.

Thus, trust lies at the basis of regulatory transgenerational actions, whereas conservative transgenerational actions are founded on normative bonds and systems that govern the transgenerational action and determine their conditions of possibility. In the case of conservative transgenerational actions, norms step in where the relationship of trust, by its very nature, is lacking.

Regulatory transgenerational actions and solidarity

We have seen how conservative transgenerational actions expressly serve the interests of the agents who originate them, while regulatory transgenerational actions serve the interests of equity and justice, where the intention is to regulate what would otherwise not be regulated, and balance out what would otherwise be biased in favour of a specific generation. It is worthwhile asking now whether such actions have anything to do with the concept of solidarity. In other words, whether such actions promote or require solidarity.

As I will now explain, transgenerational actions do not necessarily come with an attitude of solidarity, although it can be the case in both conservative and regulatory transgenerational actions. Solidarity is a complex notion that does not depend on the notion of justice, or on the idea that people tied by a relationship of solidarity pursue just ends – members of mafia clans show such close solidarity that it is the very basis of the existence of the clan itself, and solidarity is not the same as loyalty.[31]

Solidarity is a disposition for action, often a political action, by an agent who acts 'in the stead' of other agents, for which the action is conceived as a surrogate for the action of those others. With solidarity, agents first choose whose side to take and then engage with the arguments advanced by that side, where as I have said, those arguments are not necessarily founded on any sense of justice. Furthermore, unlike in the case of loyalty, solidarity relationships do not imply a dependency between the person entering the solidarity relationship and the person with whom they are solidary. In other words, they enter the solidarity relationship for a series of reasons r, where such reasons can be just or unjust, and are independent of any specific agent.

Avery Kolers provides some very clear examples.[32] Let us suppose we live in a country under apartheid rule. A coloured woman boards a bus and sits down. A few stops later, a white woman boards the bus, which by now has filled up, and there is nowhere to sit. At that point, the conductor asks the coloured woman to stand and give up her seat. She refuses and the police force her off the bus. Showing solidarity with the coloured woman would probably mean choosing to alight the bus with her – it means deciding to act by alighting a bus on which you have the right to continue travelling.

We could also imagine another variant, where a person witnessing the scene chooses to stand up and defend the unfortunate woman. If the person is solidary and the coloured woman asks him to return to his seat, regardless of his moral sense and his beliefs about human rights, the person will return to his seat, doing what the woman has asked him to do. Therefore, showing solidarity means taking up somebody's side and being willing to act on their terms, or as they would have acted or would like us to act; and if they ask us to, it means changing our action plans, even for reasons that we do not agree with.

The above demonstrates how transgenerational action implies a plurality of agents, separated by a certain distance of time. Thus, I suppose the following schema, whereby a transgenerational action is initiated by an agent or a group of agents (S_i). It is plausible to think that the agents (S_i) are motivated by a series of reasons (r), which have predisposed them to take the action and led them to act. We can suppose that the agents who take up the transgenerational action (S_e) take the side of S_i, and thus act, in consideration of (r), as (S_i) wants or would like them to act. Therefore, (S_i) leave it to (S_e) to act in their stead, according to their will.

Let us consider five scenarios of transgenerational actions, three conservative and two regulatory.

The first scenario [1] outlines a conservative transgenerational action. A state is going through a period of strong economic growth and relative development. The prime minister of the country, however, is eager to consolidate her electoral support, as times are tough from a political point of view, with serious tensions on the rise – an armed guerrilla group is threatening the political and institutional stability of the country. The situation leads the government to adopt an executive decree encouraging the early retirement of public sector workers, where women with children can retire on a pension after little more than fourteen years of work, and men after around twenty years of work. The measure is widely popular with voters but smacks of social injustice, as a large number of workers will be supported by state pensions, incurring huge costs for the public purse. As a result of the policy decision, public debt will rise, as will the debt burden that future generations (S_e, in our schema) will have to bear. The costs, however, will be twofold, in terms of the expense to keep the system in place, as well as the rights of new generations, whose pension benefits will predictably be lower than the benefits enjoyed by the previous generations.

Let us now imagine a second scenario [2] similar to the first, but with the introduction of a key variant. In this scenario, the social situation is relatively stable – no social crisis or security tensions, but rather a condition of relative social peace. In this context, the government is confident and wishes to consolidate its approval by promoting the well-being of the citizens who have voted for it, so it introduces a pension reform along the lines of the executive decree described in scenario [1]. Even in this case, we have a political decision that gives rise to a precise transgenerational action – the reform of the pension system – introduced by (S_i), which will be continued, or reformed in turn, by (S_e). The set of reasons motivating the action of (S_i) has to do with maintaining popular approval and promoting the well-being of the people of (S_i). Once again, the transgenerational action initiated by (S_i) is of a conservative nature, and its impacts will clearly be similar to those of the first scenario, in terms of a disequilibrium between generations. Unlike the first scenario, however, no reason that is not of a merely conservative nature could have induced (S_i) to adopt that specific transgenerational action.

Now for a third scenario [3], which once again concerns the reform of the pension system. In this case, the country is enjoying a historical moment of relative peace and prosperity, where greater and more widely distributed wealth, the consolidation of the welfare system and higher education levels have progressively and considerably lengthened the average life expectancy of citizens. People are living longer and on average the quality of life is improving. In such a context, and aware that such decisions in theory could prove quite unpopular, the government has introduced measures aimed at lengthening the working life of its citizens, which means that people will retire later in life. Thus, the government has chosen to promote pension reforms that, unlike the decrees enacted by the governments in scenarios [1] and [2], call on citizens to work a little longer to secure benefits in the form of the sustainability of the pension system and in terms of fairer intergenerational relations. Given the consistent ageing of the population, the raising of the retirement age will help avert the clear disadvantages that future generations would otherwise face in terms of their rights and entitlements. The system will therefore be balanced and fair (or fairer) over the long term, which, as one of its side effects, will promote greater social stability. The transgenerational action in this scenario is of a regulatory nature. In a situation of prosperity and well-being, the citizens of our imaginary state plan to extend the sphere of rights they enjoy and make it possible for future generations to enjoy those same rights.

The fourth scenario [4] contemplates a change in the economic state of affairs. In this scenario, the economy is not growing, but stagnant, and the country is going through a period in which wealth per capita is not growing in any significant way. Yet, despite the situation, the government decides to push ahead with plans to reform the pension system. Public sector workers will be able to retire early, after fourteen years of work for women and twenty years for men. The economy continues to stagnate and unproductive public expenditure rises – as presumably will public debt, given that debt will be needed to service the system, in the short term at least. The policy decision of the government in scenario [4] serves to win votes, thus it is clearly a conservative transgenerational action, whereby (S_i) acts to implement pension reforms designed to win popular approval for the government.

Let us now return to the question of solidarity. In the four scenarios I have set out so far, is it possible for (S_e) to show solidarity? The answer is yes, in all four cases, albeit for different reasons.

In scenario [1], (S_e) may take the side of (S_i), if it agrees with the political reasons that led (S_i) to avert the potential collapse of the state and its institutions. Alternatively, (S_e) may not approve the substance of the decisions taken by (S_i), on the grounds, perhaps, that (S_i) ought to have chosen other means of strengthening social and political unity, for instance, by investing in the cultural sphere and development. Nevertheless, (S_e) may appreciate the underlying motivations of (S_i) and choose to act as (S_i) wanted, by committing to support the expense of the new reformed pension system.

In scenario [2], there were many different options from which (S_i) could have chosen. Economic growth and social stability would easily have allowed the government to plan longer-term policies and ask its citizens to make a small sacrifice for the greater good of consolidating its institutions. Yet, (S_i) decided to do otherwise, to consolidate its popular approval. As such, (S_e) would have quite a number of good reasons to demand a re-examination of those pension reforms, by arguing the point, for instance, of intergenerational equity, as the reformed system will in all likelihood produce social inequity. Nevertheless, it could be imagined that the social agents belonging to (S_e) agree with the populist vision that led (S_i) to act as it did, and with the idea that ultimately political action is largely about consolidating the support of voters.

Scenario [3] instead had as its outcome a regulatory transgenerational action. In a situation of widespread growth and substantial social stability, (S_i) committed to strengthening its institutions and furthering social stability by making choices in pursuit of an equilibrium and greater justice between generations over the long term. That is why it chose to adopt a system that raised the retirement age, without leaving behind people in situations of particular hardship. The political design of (S_i) focused on building a society that takes account of transgenerational equilibria and intergenerational justice, while offering safeguards for the weak and disadvantaged. Such a choice will help stabilize the functioning of institutions in the long term, which in turn, will create better conditions to foster both economic and social development policies.[33] In such a context, (S_e) will support the reasons behind such governmental decisions and show solidarity in its approach, acting as (S_i) would like it to act and pushing ahead with the implementation of policy decisions that add greater scope to political action.

Scenario [4] once again gives an example of a conservative transgenerational action. Economic stagnation is holding back growth, for which per capita incomes are dwindling. The government has at best a short-term vision of the country's future, choosing to hold onto power by adopting stop-gap measures of limited scope, but which will clearly be popular with voters. Thus, one of the first measures was to tinker with the pension system so as to lower the retirement age. The social agents of (S_e) may largely share the populist vision that led (S_i) to initiate the transgenerational action and agree that the consolidation of popular approval and, specifically, the well-being of the immediate electorate is effectively the primary objective of government. As such it will be solidary with (S_i) and voluntarily commit to the transgenerational action.

Now for a fifth and final scenario [5] as an instance of a regulatory transgenerational action. In this scenario, the economic cycle is negative and the economy is in recession. Nevertheless, the social climate is positive, showing substantial confidence and widespread belief in the idea that high levels of cultural and scientific education are the key to improving quality of life in terms of opportunities and growth. Building on the nationwide sense of solidarity, the government adopts longer-term economic policies that aim to improve the level of social justice and the stability of institutions over time. Accordingly, it adopts pension measures designed to allow people willing to remain in the labour force to work longer. Such measures clearly aim, among other things, to achieve greater intergenerational justice. In such a context, (S_e) will support the reasons behind such governmental decisions and be solidary in its approach, acting as (S_i) would like (S_e) to act and pushing ahead with the implementation of policy decisions that add longer-term scope to political action.

These five scenarios demonstrate two things in particular. The first is the difference, in practice, between conservative and regulatory transgenerational actions; the second is how solidarity, which is perfectly possible in all the scenarios, is not a sufficient condition to promote regulatory transgenerational actions. Or in other words, the fact that all five scenarios are, in theory, compatible with an attitude of solidarity implies that solidarity is not a sufficient condition for transgenerational actions to be accomplished. Thus, another type of condition must be necessary for the adoption of criteria of justice.

As such, I believe it would be useful to explore what would happen in the five scenarios outlined above if no solidarity were shown by (S_e) in its response. In scenarios [1], [2] and [4], the most likely outcome is that S_e would decide not to take up the transgenerational action, demanding instead a re-examination of the reasons behind it and the principles underpinning it. Such a re-examination could be achieved in two ways:

1. by redefining the meaning of the transgenerational action and, as a consequence, how the pension reforms were structured within those scenarios. One outcome of such a review would probably be an overhaul of the characteristics of the system. That would imply that the pension system – a factor of equilibrium for the social systems of advanced democracies – produces inequity and hence instability; or
2. more radically, by overturning the decisions of (S_i), on the grounds that they were unjust and founded, in turn, on unjust grounds. Such an argument, however, would raise rather important issues concerning justice, for is it just – and if it is, to what extent – to unilaterally reconsider a compact, or a part of a compact, that a state, through its government, has made with its citizens?

In scenarios [3] and [5], any lack of solidarity shown by (S_e) would in practice result in the suspension of the regulatory transgenerational action and, predictably, the adoption of more conservative positions. Thus, what emerges, overall, is that solidarity, being neutral with respect to the purpose of a transgenerational action, is not a sufficient criterion to motivate the adoption of regulatory transgenerational actions. Yet, it is precisely regulatory transgenerational actions that help shape the construction of a society that is fairer and more appreciative of social relationships that extend in time.

Objections and replies

Let us now look at some possible objections to the perspective I have outlined so far.

The first has to do with a certain ontological overabundance implicit in our arguments. It can be summed up in the doubt, are we really sure there is a theoretical convenience in including this sort of entity, namely transgenerational actions, in our ontological inventory of actions? In other words, if, on the one hand, it is rather easy to grasp the difference between a gesture and an action and there are good reasons to support the idea that group actions exist, on the other, there can be some scepticism about the opportunity of including transgenerational actions in our catalogue.

Given that, as Ascombe suggests, actions are widely determined by the description we give of them, privileging a diachronic understanding of them and committing to an assessment of their consequences gives rise to two considerations to think about. First, it permits us to grasp a fundamental element, which is that social structures aim to endure in time, for a period that is virtually infinite. Time is not an ancillary factor in the determination of a social equilibrium, as societies often tend to be conservative in relation to the dynamics that constitute them and the power relations that innervate them. Thus, changes unfold over time intervals that are generally quite long or, in contrast, by means of sudden episodes that can be driven by various causes but are radical enough to profoundly alter existing arrangements. Therefore, time counts for much and should be given due consideration.

The second consideration is that the perspective allows us, more than others, to put the consequences of particular social actions into better focus. That is, it brings to the fore the significance and the importance of the consequences of those actions that have an impact over time on others, or on the social reality we have constructed. In short, it is an approach to thinking about social reality that places the notion of responsibility at the centre.[34] But it is a type of responsibility that clearly will become evident only after a certain amount of time – a peculiarity that generally encourages a tendency not to recognize the normative character of that responsibility, with the result that, in a great many cases, it winds up being disregarded.

There is, however, a further aspect of the matter that it is important to remember: consequences and responsibilities are significant not only for the lives of the people involved in processes of this kind but also for the life of society itself. If the importance and dynamics of the transgenerational plane are not suitably recognized, it is the very existence of social institutions that will become troublesome, in terms of the prospects for economic development, social justice and, ultimately, our welfare.

Essentially, therefore, our argument is that three simple moves suffice to equip our social theories more effectively than they have been to date. The first move is to consider the development of societies over time as a decisive element not only for understanding history but also for formulating hypotheses able to steer the future. The second move lies in considering the importance of the concept of future generations and treating them as abstract artefacts whose form of existence entails the movement from potentiality to actuality. Much like fictional characters, future generations are distinguished by a hybrid form of being, where we introduce them into our world catalogue in order to imagine stories and create worlds. Unlike fictional characters, however, sooner or later future generations will exist in space and time. It is that particular property that radically changes things and that should be taken as a reminder to be especially prudent when undertaking actions that will entail the participation of future generations. For it is entirely impossible to do something that could cause any true harm to the young Count Bezúkhov, whereas it is highly possible to commit actions that will seriously damage the possibilities open to a future generation, along with the social context in which it will live. Once again, the future counts and cannot be ignored.

The third move consists in taking responsibility for the consequences of social actions, including therein transgenerational actions, which from this perspective, are the most difficult to deal with as they imply a certain predictive capacity, while also requiring an express commitment to steering the future and taking responsibility for it. We need to try and steer what might be so that when it effectively comes to be, the life of the people who will come after us is not suffocated by an unacceptable and unjust burden. That would serve to guarantee both justice and an equilibrium between generations, elements that are essential for a society to endure in conditions of social and economic prosperity.

Another important objection concerns the level of granularity to apply to transgenerational actions, or which actions we should include in this particular class. All social actions? Or some more than others? For if we consider all or the majority of social actions from a transgenerational perspective, it may overly complicate the chances of action and choice in the social and political sphere. In short, all this may help us solve the problem we are addressing, but it also raises new issues. An excessively inclusive approach would have the consequence of forcing us to develop an anti-economical theory that would demand an assessment of every single social action in relation to its consequences – which is arguably neither useful nor necessary.

Finally we come to the matter of choice. What types of action can be considered usefully from a transgenerational perspective, and why? Any exclusion obviously entails some risk, first and foremost the risk of underestimation or misunderstanding – that is true especially when it comes to envisaging the long-term consequences of our actions. Ultimately, it is a matter of drawing up a list that makes no claim to be exhaustive. We can identify spheres of social life that are particularly sensitive, and which therefore deserve a certain attentiveness, as otherwise social equilibria would tend to become progressively more complicated. Here are some issues that strike me as being particularly significant: climate change; the formation of public debt; the sustainability of welfare systems, in particular the sustainability of pension systems; and labour market equilibria, in a historical period in which average life expectancy has grown significantly, while birth rates are declining in almost every Western economy. All these cases raise issues of equity and justice that can only be fully appreciated with reference to the long, or longer term, and by looking at the consequences of transgenerational social actions.

The final chapter stops and examines some of those cases to explore what it means, in practice, to take responsibility or decline responsibility for transgenerationality.

4

A Few Applications

The case of Venice: From transgenerational inclusion to fall

If we acknowledge the particular structure that transgenerational actions have, then we must also acknowledge that one particular type, regulatory transgenerational actions, aims to support an inclusive strategy that strengthens cooperation and engagement between generations. Regulatory transgenerational actions, when implemented on the broader scale, enable transgenerational policies that we define as regulatory to be pursued.

So let us look at how regulatory transgenerational policies serve as a means to strengthen inclusion processes that generally promote and intensify social and economic growth. It is clear how the capacity to endure in time is not per se synonymous with social growth and development. On the contrary, history gives us examples of quite the opposite. In general, healthy societies display three characteristics: (1) they build institutions and economies that are inclusive, and not merely extractive; (2) they organize power in centralized and efficient ways that resist the disgregation that tends to be produced by local and corporative forms of sub-power; and finally, (3) they foster technological innovation, a process that is not simple to manage, given its intrinsically ambiguous character – something which led Joseph Schumpeter to define it as 'creative destruction'.[1] Technological innovation enables new ways of seeing the world and new possibilities for action. At the same time, however, it rapidly renders old institutions and legacy practices obsolete, excluding from the production process a great many people, who end up on the margins of the system. The creative revolution is, therefore, a complex process that brings benefits but also massive costs. Thus, it must be steered and managed with awareness by institutions.

The distinction I mentioned between extractive institutions and economies and inclusive institutions and economies deserves particular attention. Extractive institutions and economies seek to extract as much wealth as possible over a certain time from a specific context. They are, in short, conservative. In practice, the objective of extractive economies lies in producing wealth in the interests of hegemonic power groups that, on the whole, seek to preserve their power. In contrast, inclusive institutions and economies seek to broaden as far as possible the distribution of wealth and build a system of power as inclusive as possible.

It is not infrequent that rather long-serving institutions shift from one form to the other. Of the extensive list of case studies analysed by Acemoglu and Robinson[2] to illustrate the difference between extractive economies and inclusive economies, the example of the Venetian Republic and its rise and fall is enlightening. The prestige of the Serenissima began its rise around the year 1000. After a period of profound decline following the collapse of the Roman Empire, Venice recovered to make the most of the growing stability of the European economy, underpinned by the restoration of centralized political power under Charlemagne. It was then that the Venetian Republic really took advantage of its uniquely promising geographical position, giving unprecedented new impulse to its trading activities. Around 1050, the city could boast a booming economy and a population of around 45,000 people. By 1200, its population had grown to 70,000, to then more than double by the year 1330 to 110,000.

The turning point for the republic's fortunes came with the introduction of contractual innovations – hence by means of a legal instrument – that proved capable of injecting major stimulus into trade growth, while guaranteeing broad social mobility. That legal instrument was the *commenda*. The term *commenda* covers various legal instruments, all of which share the idea of commending something to someone – whether it is a person, in the sense of a person recommending his or her candidate to another (the *commendatio romana*), or a vacant ecclesiastical benefice, entrusted in custody to a layperson or the holder of a connected office, or finally goods or money, committed by a commender to a commendator under a specific business arrangement. It was the latter type of *commenda*, as a business arrangement, that proved decisive for the extraordinary rise of the city.

The *commenda* enabled the trading capacity of Venice to be expanded greatly, as the structure of the contract opened up participation in trade to a vast part of the population, thus fostering upward social mobility and transgenerational inclusion. Typically, every trade mission was governed by a *commenda* contract that lasted only for the duration of the mission itself. One of the partners was sedentary and provided the capital, while the other travelled with the merchandise. Such an arrangement permitted even those without capital to invest to engage in trade, which evidently favoured the less affluent and young people. Profits were shared on the basis of the type of *commenda* contract made. If it was unilateral, the sedentary partner financed 100 per cent of the mission and received 75 per cent of the profits. Otherwise, the sedentary partner put up 67 per cent of the capital, to then receive 50 per cent of the profits.

Documents from the era show not only how effective the contractual instrument was in helping generate wealth but also its role in promoting upward social mobility and a truly inclusive economy. The *commenda* contract contributed to the greater distribution of wealth and a better capacity for inclusion in Venetian society. It led institutions to change and evolve towards greater inclusiveness, becoming themselves more open. The election of the doge demonstrates this. Initially, the doge was elected for life by the General Assembly. Although the Assembly was a general gathering of all citizens, in practice it was controlled by a handful of noble families. Over time, the powers of the doge were progressively limited. As of 1032, the doge was elected by a Ducal Council, whose chief task was to limit certain of the doge's powers significantly. The effect of such checks and balances on power was to further expand the trading capacity of the Venetian Republic, to the point that in 1082, it was granted permission to establish a trading colony in no less than Constantinople, which soon numbered over ten thousand Venetians.

The assassination of the doge in 1171 ushered in a series of sweeping reforms, the most important of which was the establishment of the Great Council, which would become the key political institution of the republic, with the doge chosen from its members. Although all social classes were represented on the Great Council, in practice it was controlled by a fairly small core of merchant families. It was those families who in 1297 imposed the Serrata, which in practice made it possible to enter the assembly only by hereditary right. Those and other institutional reforms ultimately aimed to restrict the power of the doge in various ways and concentrate power in the republic in the hands of a somewhat restricted circle of families. The decisions also came with the introduction of a series of key technical and legal innovations, such as the creation of independent magistrates, courts, an appellate court and the institution of new forms of private law, which among other things affected the development of banks – Venice, in fact, was home to one of the earliest modern banking systems.

If we observe the political and economic history of the Venetian Republic more closely, a few things can be noted. The first is how the inclusive economy so distinctly fostered by the development of the *commenda* was no stranger to tensions unleashed by the creative destruction so often entailed by major development processes. Creative destruction opens up paths for social mobility and widens the base of wealth, but it also creates social tensions as the classes that hold power generally do not want to share it or see it eroded. That was basically the reason that led to the Serrata in 1297, when the Great Council essentially closed its ranks. The Serrata, however, came after several phases of expansion, which saw the council's inclusiveness progressively grow through the cooption of an increasingly greater number of citizens, expanding its ranks from an initial 450 members to around 1,500 at its greatest point of expansion.

Venice's political closure came hand in hand with an economic closure that paved the way for the city's slow decline. The first step came with the abolition of the *commenda* contract, the very institution that had contributed to Venice's prosperity. Its abolition made access to trade more difficult for the same bourgeoisie that had fuelled the economic growth of La Serenissima. The scrapping of the *commenda* effectively crippled the city, completely enfeebling its capacity to pursue an inclusive and transgenerational economic policy, to the advantage of rentier positions and their fortification. The strategy was further entrenched by the substantial nationalization of trade in 1314, and then the introduction of heavy taxes in 1324 on individuals wishing to engage in trade. The outcome of the two decisions was to steer the Serenissima's politics and economy in an extractive direction on the whole, showing a complete disregard for the duties and obligations tied to the transgenerational social actions that the government of the Venetian Republic had formerly pursued.

Venice's case is instructive as it allows us to reflect on a number of key points. To begin with, it allows us to observe how the city grew in terms of its wealth, population and institutional variety and complexity, so long as it was willing and able to implement policies that embraced transgenerational integration and social inclusion. On the contrary, its decline began once it chose to close its institutions, making intra-social and transgenerational cooperation trickier and more complex. In short, it was when Venetian society began to crystallize around legacy practices and established wealth and to neglect any incentive for economic development policies, raising hurdles to social inclusion (especially generational inclusion), that the city's destiny began its turnaround for the worse.

Venice's history shows how complex institutions can go through alternating stages, and how the difference between an inclusive policy approach and an extractive policy approach can lie in the simple adoption of a legal instrument that fosters collaboration, as was effectively the case with the *commenda* contract. The moment Venetian citizens chose to preserve the status quo and crystallize traditional power arrangements, the city fell into progressive decline, transforming itself into what effectively today is a stunningly beautiful open-air museum.

Venice continues to exist, but its soul is by no means what it once was. Now its wealth is largely extractive in nature, in the sense it is generated by exploiting the city's monumental legacy and tourist potential, without any real vision of what its future might be. Moreover, mass tourism in the numbers that pour into Venice every year is of no help in preserving that monumental legacy or the city itself – policy decisions for the most part are oriented towards generating wealth from the continued mass exploitation of its monumental assets in ways that, with time, may undermine the city's very existence. Such an intensive form of extraction shows little to no regard for the transgenerational dimension of a heritage that is a common good.

An example of transgenerational inequity: Pensions

For a certain part of its history at least, Venice proved its ability to be inclusive by promoting transgenerationality as a factor for integration. Let us now turn to an example of what it means to completely disregard transgenerationality, in both its rationale and practices, namely a *non*-transgenerational approach, this time focusing on the world of work.

Much like the art world, or the world of finance, the world of work is a rather vague entity that is made up of a vast variety of agents who are not always necessarily the same, and whose roles and tasks largely vary. Generally speaking, the world of work encompasses all those people who are either employed, or unemployed, or seeking employment, or have given up seeking employment, or are employed to help others find employment, as well as public and private organizations that employ workers, and others.

The transgenerational relationship can be found in two forms in the labour market: in the transfer of skills and knowledge from one generation to another and in the 'collaboration' required between those in gainful employment and those who after years of gainful employment retire on an old-age pension. This section will focus on the latter, namely old-age pensions.

As widely noted, the benefits paid by the state to pensioners are funded by active workers. That systems produces a transgenerational chain that is virtually perfect, whereby each link in the imaginary chain first gives to others and then takes from others what it needs to live in proportion to the wealth that it itself has contributed to creating. This specific structure of our society openly acknowledges the importance of the transgenerational bond, as each new generation takes up the duty of supporting the old, giving a mature expression of what it means to be human, namely taking care of the older, and hence more exposed, members of society.

That, at least, is the general framework. For if such a form of transgenerational support constitutes one of the most important elements of the welfare state, its implementation is not infrequently liable to create forms of injustice, of which transgenerational injustice is arguably one of the most important. As an example we will look at one Italian affair, which is rather significant from at least two points of view. First, it clearly demonstrates what the consequences are of political choices and conduct that ignore the issue of transgenerationality; and second, it similarly demonstrates how much resistance there is to the application of transgenerational policies.

But first things first. The history of the Italian social security system is a history of the numerous reforms which the system has gone through.[3] Here I will briefly retrace the fundamental stages. The Italian social security system was first set up in 1898, with a view to protecting the welfare of workers in the event of invalidity and in their old age. In 1919, invalidity and old-age insurance became compulsory for all private-sector employees, and invalidity and old-age pensions were instituted. Also in 1919, unemployment insurance became mandatory. Between 1927 and 1941, a state redundancy fund was created to offer key wage protection for workers who lose their jobs through redundancy; the retirement age to qualify for an old-age pension was raised to sixty years for men and fifty-five years for women; and a survivor's pension was introduced. Between 1968 and 1972, the defined benefit system on which pensions were based was changed to a defined contribution system, and alongside the old-age pension, a social security pension was introduced for citizens over the age of sixty-five on low incomes. In 1992, lawmakers raised the minimum retirement age to sixty-five years for both men and women, and the insurance requirement to a minimum of twenty years of contributions. As of 1995, a series of corrective measures introduced new bases for the calculation of old-age pensions – the amount of contributions paid over the person's working years, the expected duration of the pension entitlement and life expectancy – which took the important step of considering the longer average life span of the population.

Thus, although the central importance of the pension scheme has not been lost, the underlying idea since the mid-1990s has been that longer life spans should affect how pension benefits are calculated. For, in theory at least, if people can look forward to a longer life and have access to a better quality of life, then it can only be hoped they will work longer. That, at least, is the general idea, with due exception made for certain categories of workers whose jobs are particularly arduous or hazardous.

Yet, Italy also offers an exemplary case of a pension reform whose measures did not respect the criteria of transgenerational justice, or those of plain common sense. The year was 1973 when the Italian government, led by the then prime minister Mariano Rumor, introduced a reform package that would come to be dubbed the 'baby pensions' measure, passed by Presidential Decree (DPR 1092, in particular Article 42).[4] The measure afforded extremely generous pension conditions for certain categories of public sector workers, by setting the insurance requirement for an old-age pension at fourteen years, six months and one day of contributions for married women with children, at twenty years of contributions for other public sector workers and at twenty-five years of contributions for local government workers. The early retirement opportunity was taken up by around 400,000 people, entailing an annual pension outlay that has been estimated at 7.5 billion euros per year.

The 'baby pensions' measure was repealed in 1992 by the Amato government as part of its belt-tightening response to a currency crisis that Italy was facing. The emergency fiscal measures were based on an overhaul of the pension system, the introduction of a property tax on homes and a one-off levy on bank current accounts. The pension measures introduced by the Rumor government entailed significant consequences that would persist into the long term. The first was the impact on public spending, as the pension outlay rose staggeringly to cover benefits paid to people still in the prime of their working years, when they could otherwise have easily continued working for another twenty-five years, adding to the productivity and wealth of the country. Then there were the consequences in terms of social justice and intergenerational justice.

As concerns social justice, it should be noted how those pension benefits were, for the most part, reserved to public sector employees, whose jobs are generally less arduous and less hazardous than those of other workers. From that point of view, many categories of workers were excluded, despite arguably having a greater entitlement to early retirement. Then there is the aspect of the financial support the measures aimed to offer women with children. Such income support raised evident issues for female independence, as ultimately it ended up limiting the possibilities open to women, by encouraging them to return to the yoke of household management and to the care of family members by providing a state-funded pension. Rather than investing public money in the creation of social services to help women balance work and family obligations, the government instead chose to adopt an economic means of perpetuating a traditional social model that greatly restricted the social role of women to the household. Thus, improper use was made of a welfare tool to defend and protect a conservative and extractive social model.

But that is not all. The measures also entailed major consequences on the transgenerational plane. For the generations that followed those that benefited from the Rumor reform were not only compelled to bear part of the burden of the exorbitant cost incurred by those 'baby pensions', which would continue to be paid by the state for a great many years with the lengthening of average life expectancies, but they would see their own entitlements eroded greatly, both in the lower income their pensions would offer them and the higher retirement age set to access them. Along with other factors, those 'baby pensions' ultimately contributed to undermining the sustainability of the pension system within the macroeconomic framework of the country, which would lead successive Italian governments to tighten the rules and adopt a more restrictive system, in terms of the benefits afforded – in practice, lower pension payouts – and the conditions of eligibility, with the retirement age raised considerably.

Thus, the two major consequences of the adoption of the 'baby pensions' system were that it contributed to putting the sustainability of Italian welfare at risk, and it created a wide gap in transgenerational justice. Such a system, with the characteristics it had, could only have been sustainable on the conditions of a growing resident population and sustained levels of economic growth. Instead, the opposite happened. Population growth in Italy began slowing down in the 1970s, and flattened out in the 1980s, with the lowest point reached in 2017 (see Figures 2 and 3).

Figure 4 shows the statistical forecast of demographic trends through to 2065.

In such a framework, it is easy to appreciate that gross domestic product has not fared much better, with the debt/GDP ratio showing constant growth from the 1970s through to 1994, when it dropped significantly, only to start rising again as of 2008 (see Figure 5).[5]

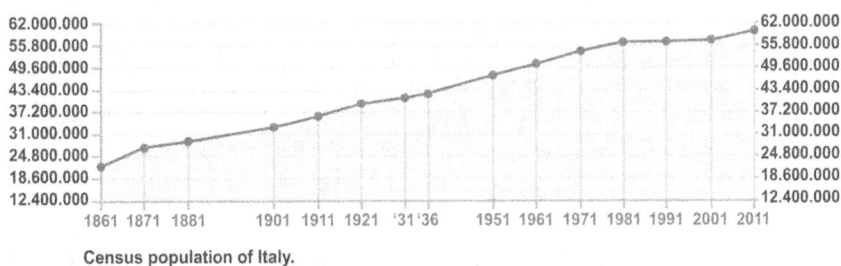

Census population of Italy.

Figure 2 Resident population trend in Italy: 1861–2011. *Source:* ISTAT figures.

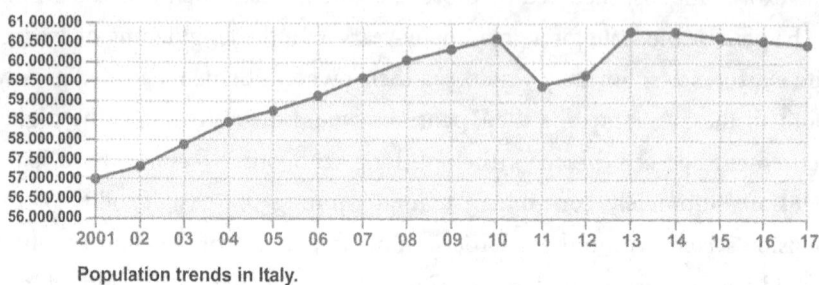

Figure 3 Resident population trend in Italy: 2001–2017. *Source:* ISTAT figures.

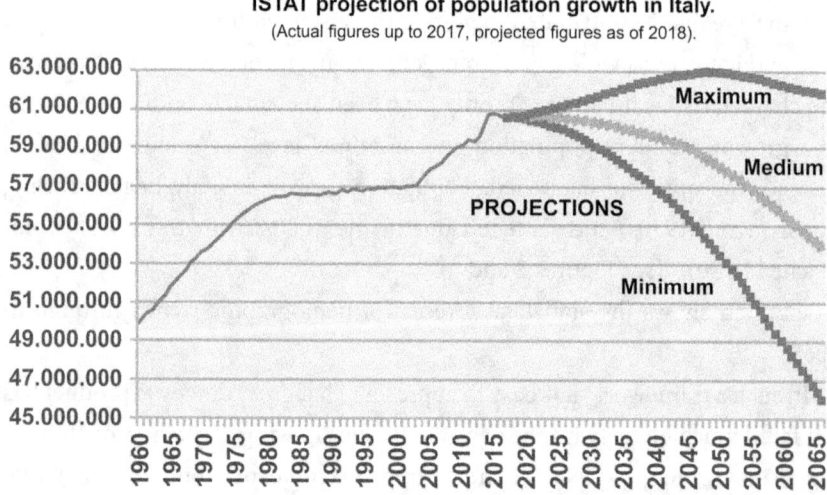

Figure 4 The chart shows the trend in the overall resident population in Italy (Italian and foreign nationals) at 1 January of every year from 1960 to 2017, as calculated by ISTAT. As of 2018, three demographic projections developed by ISTAT through to 2065 are reported, showing the median value and two projections based on the highest and lowest growth scenarios developed by ISTAT. *Source:* Department for Economic Policy Planning and Coordination (http://www.programmazioneeconomica.gov.it/2018/12/20/andamenti-lungo-periodo-economia-italiana/#Debito%20pubblico).

Figure 6 shows the trend in public expenditure on welfare benefits and pension payments, which is similarly significant. The bottom line clearly reveals the progressive fall in the number of public sector employees, whereas

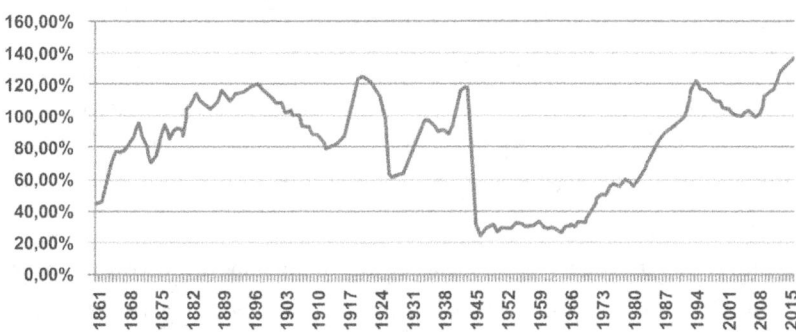

Figure 5 Italy Debt/GDP % (1861–2015). *Source:* Department for Economic Policy Planning and Coordination (http://www.programmazioneeconomica.gov. it/2018/12/20/andamenti-lungo-periodo-economia-italiana/#Debito%20pubblico).

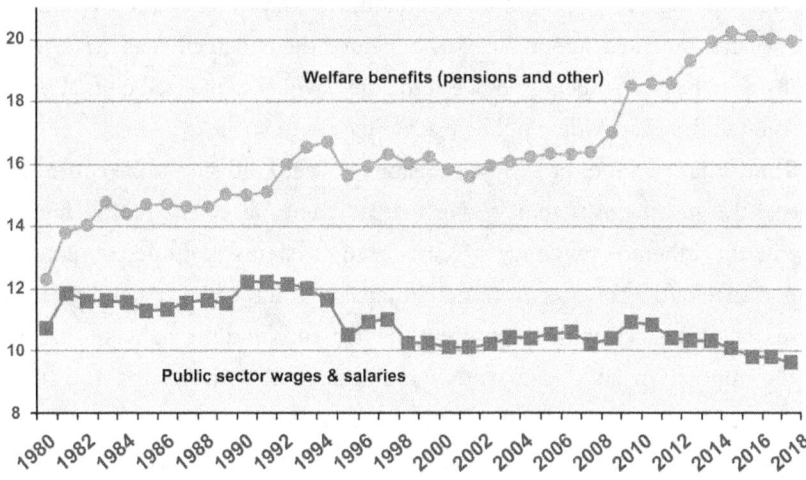

Figure 6 The chart shows the trend in public expenditure, as a % of GDP, on public sector wages and salaries and on cash welfare benefits, of which the outlay on pensions (old-age and social security) constitutes the biggest share. *Source:* Department for Economic Policy Planning and Coordination (http://www.programmazioneeconomica. gov.it/2018/12/20/andamenti-lungo-periodo-economia-italiana/#Debito%20pubblico).

the top line shows the progressive rise, as of the 1980s, in expenditure on welfare benefits and pensions.

The macroeconomic picture that emerges from this overview is clearly not the most encouraging. Cross-referencing the data reported in the ISTAT charts, it can be concluded that since the 1970s, Italy's debt burden has progressively worsened due to high levels of public spending (where pension outlays represent one the biggest expenditure items). That has come with a marked fall in birth rates, significantly longer life expectancy for the population and a progressive drop in GDP.

At this point, the question becomes, could all that have been foreseen back in 1973, the year Rumor pushed through his reform package? As Hans Jonas teaches us,[6] when dealing with transgenerational issues – and pensions are a supremely transgenerational matter – the least favourable predictions should always be given serious consideration. Efforts must be focused not so much on predicting the future, as complicated as that is, but on steering it through sensible policy decisions. Mariano Rumor and his government, along with the parliamentarians elected to that legislature, chose to pursue what was evidently a conservative and populist approach, by opting for an economic policy of an extractive nature – the pension measures adopted clearly benefited the Italian citizens living in the 1970s, and the government in office at the time, which capitalized on that policy decision to draw an evident political advantage at the polls.

Thus, it is crucial to note how decisions of that kind should be considered one of the mortal risks that Western democracies face. The reason for that lies in the inherent tendency of democratic systems to underestimate the importance of the transgenerational dimension and the issues that dimension raises. Democracies, in fact, represent the demands and the rights of that part of the population entitled to vote, which means that the young and future generations, for instance, often only have access to indirect or marginal forms of representation. Thus, it easily emerges how democratic systems take into account the synchronic plane first of all, while for obvious reasons they are less attentive of assessments from a diachronic perspective. Civil rights movements have done much to broaden the franchise considerably and extend political representation, such as in the case of women's suffrage. Nevertheless, the problem of the extension of political representation continues to represent an open issue.

The lengthening of average life expectancies in all Western democracies raises a concrete question concerning the average age of those entitled to vote, which is progressively rising. That means that the interests expressed by a wide part of the electorate are largely those typical of senior citizens. Moreover, the amount of public money earmarked for health costs (a system that senior citizens typically rely on greatly) and to cover pension outlays is growing constantly. That obviously generates social tensions, as public spending is perceived to be substantially imbalanced and unjust.[7]

To some extent, therefore, democratic systems appear to raise rather urgent questions about justice. The criticalities in terms of transgenerational justice, in turn, seem to determine similarly important criticalities in terms of social justice. In short, democracies are not naturally sensitive to transgenerational issues, which in the long term generally causes major problems. Or more specifically, societies where the average age of voters is rising considerably, as is happening in nearly all Western democracies, and which show little sensitivity to transgenerational issues run the serious risk of implementing decisions that are inequitable in a major way, unless specific corrective measures are put in place.[8]

Governments and institutions that choose to pursue extractive economic and social policies are characterized by their production of a well-being that generally is limited, as such policies tend to enrich certain social groups without generating true development. As such, growth in extractive economies depends on the continuation of policies to incentivize development. Once they dry up, the process comes to a halt.[9] In the case of the Rumor pension reform, that specific policy decision – clearly of an extractive nature and contrary to the most basic principles of protecting transgenerationality – brought undue and unfair advantages to a part of the Italian population. Political actions of that kind can only be read in terms of the electoral support they guarantee, in societies that are substantially unprepared for the task of steering the future.

To continue with the Rumor decree, the consequences of that policy decision were of two orders. First of all, it altered the productive capacity of the country, which prematurely lost a significant part of its workforce. Secondly, the generational balance was significantly tipped in favour of some few thousand people. Policy decisions, especially those of an emergency nature, should be assessed in terms of their impacts in both the short term and the long term –

decisions such as the Rumor pension reform in the long run generate deep social tensions, and hence widespread social instability. The decisions of the Rumor government rendered Italy's future more uncertain, impoverishing it and placing social equilibria at risk. Among the main problems tied to economic policies of an extractive bent – precisely along the lines of the 'baby pensions' reform – is that in the long term, the growth generated by such policies is not sustainable because it depends on exogenous factors. Moreover, such policies create evident problems of justice, as exemplified by the Rumor reform and the patent transgenerational inequalities it highlights.

To be designed correctly, pension systems need to strike a balance between at least two different planes, namely social justice and transgenerational justice. From the point of view of social justice, assessments need to be made concerning the characteristics of different occupations, the type of physical and mental toll they take, differences in terms of gender and so on. From the point of view of transgenerational justice, it is imperative to ensure that parents and children, ideally at least, are placed in comparable positions in terms of the rights they are entitled to and the duties they are bound to.

Going completely against the current of transgenerational justice, and what can be considered simply as plain common sense, the Rumor government permitted the premature retirement of workers in certain economic segments, tied for the most part to a certain generation and to certain categories of public sector jobs. In that way, it laid the groundwork that would give rise to a situation of patent transgenerational injustice, as new generations have not only been denied the entitlements enjoyed by their parents, due to a social make-up and economic framework that in the meantime has changed dramatically, but also they have been compelled to bear the financial burden of the entitlements paid to 'baby pensioners', at the expense of their own. All that, obviously, without ever having been able to exercise any right to have their say.

Climate change: A brief history

Alongside pensions, now let us look at another domain in which transgenerational matters play a central role.

The issue of climate change is eminently transgenerational in nature. Here we will present the arguments supporting that statement by exploring what we know – mainly in terms of scientific data – about climate change and its anthropogenic causes. We will also discuss the actions that should be performed by the authorities with the power to limit, as far as possible, the as yet difficult to predict, but extremely dangerous, consequences tied to climate change. Finally, we will argue in favour of the idea that the main principle adopted to steer world climate diplomacy – the principle of common but differentiated responsibilities – needs to be paired with what we will call the principle of 'transgenerational responsibility'.

So to begin, how can climate change be conceptualized?

> Climate change is a problem of collective action, not only at the intra-generational level, but also and above all at the inter-generational level. Each generation has its reasons to maximize its emissions and pass on the their costs to future generations. According to some authors, what structurally holds back policy action against climate change is not so much international disagreement between states over how to divide up the costs and obligations [...], but rather the implicit and tacit generational agreement on the economic rationality of deferring the costs of such action as far as possible, transferring them onto future generations. After all, the latter have no way of protesting or incentivizing alternatives, either positively or negatively, and can only submit to the deferments of the present.[10]

The idea that I will argue in support of is that once social agents become transgenerational agents – namely agents who decide to pursue actions of a transgenerational scope – deferment, as exemplarily denounced by studies concerning climate change, is not a morally acceptable stance. That is true because present generations, in burdening future generations with a series of obligations, generally refuse to consider those future generations as having rights. In other words, if future generations are duty bound to pay the debt contracted by the generations that come before them, they are granted no right to demand that such debt be contracted for reasons that will bring benefits to them as well, or that the amount of debt should be sustainable. Such an attitude, which steers a great many policy decisions, should therefore be stopped, or minimized at least, in concrete policy action.

Article 3 of the 1992 United Nations Framework Convention on Climate reads:

1. The Parties should protect the climate system for the benefit of present and future generations of humankind, on the basis of equity and in accordance with their common but differentiated responsibilities and respective capabilities. Accordingly, the developed country Parties should take the lead in combating climate change and the adverse effects thereof.
2. The specific needs and special circumstances of developing country Parties, especially those that are particularly vulnerable to the adverse effects of climate change, and of those Parties, especially developing country Parties, that would have to bear a disproportionate or abnormal burden under the Convention, should be given full consideration.[11]

Protecting the climate is an obligation that binds present and future in the name of ensuring that the planet is able to survive – or in more general terms, in the name of the idea that being should generally prevail over non-being. The underlying assumption here implies two arguments, one of a metaphysical nature and another of an ontological nature. If we assume the principle that being should prevail over non-being is essentially binding, *then* the transgenerational constraint in climate matters is unavoidable. That general premiss, of a metaphysical and moral nature, must therefore lead to its necessary consequences on the ethical plane. Alongside the metaphysical argument, there is the argument concerning the ontological status of future generations. Given that we make specific demands of future generations, we treat them as an entity – an entity to which we attribute duties. Thus, it would seem necessary to treat them as an entity to which we also grant rights.

The metaphysical premiss – that being is better than non-being[12] – plays a fundamental role in the case of climate change because, as I will verify very soon, the scientific data, as complex as they are to read, all appear to point to a wide consensus in saying that if the anthropogenic impacts on the climate are not contained, humankind, whether directly or indirectly, may well find itself in a position of not being able to guarantee that being prevails over non-being in relation to the preservation of life on Earth.[13] That means the hierarchy of criteria that has long been taken into consideration in assessing climate change needs to be rethought.

An important premiss must be posed before taking our discussion further, which is that the climate has always changed. Over the course of its millennial-long history, the Earth has witnessed ceaseless transformations in its climate. That is the part of the story generally endorsed by climate revisionists, those who attempt to minimize or deny outright the active and decisive role that humans play in driving climate change. In other words – and this is the fact on which there is near complete agreement in the scientific community – climate matters have taken on a whole different connotation ever since humans, as of a certain historical era, started pursuing activities that undermine the planet's natural capacity to absorb greenhouse gases. Such activities are the unwanted consequences of actions aimed, for the most part, at industrial development and the creation of wealth. But still, they are there.

The crucial point that climate revisionists tend intentionally to underestimate is the role and weight borne by human activities in driving environmental and climate change. In other words, if it is true that the climate has always been transformed by endogenous causes tied to transformations in the 'Earth System', it is just as true that, commencing more or less as of the turn of the nineteenth century, when the effects of the first Industrial Revolution began to unfold across the major European nations, the weight of human intervention in environmental and climate change has become crucially more important and even decisive.

Climate change is an ecological phenomenon. The average surface temperature of the Earth is rising – more precisely, it is almost one degree Celsius higher than it was at the start of the nineteenth century. When scientists speak of climate change, they refer to higher concentrations of greenhouse gases in the atmosphere and a lower capacity for the Earth's natural systems to absorb those gases. For the vaster part of its history, the Earth System handled that capacity rather well, remaining largely in equilibrium. Today, that equilibrium has been undermined by causes that are, as we said, largely anthropogenic in nature. That is, they can be traced back to human action and to the prolonged and massive use of fossil fuels to power industrial processes ever since the first Industrial Revolution (dating more or less from 1760 to 1850). Those processes have significantly raised the living standards of millions of people over many generations, progressively reaching wider and wider swathes of the planet. The Industrial Revolution of the nineteenth century, as with the subsequent revolutions that have taken hold, especially in the West, involved complex processes investing a variety of different aspects of society, in many cases not without conflict.[14] In net terms, the industrialization of manufacturing activities, as well as agriculture, has helped reduce poverty greatly, bringing progressive improvement to living standards and considerably lengthening the life expectancy of people.

The transgenerational nature of the industrialization process is quite evident, given that it unfolded over a rather lengthy period of time. In many ways, it is not yet over, considering we are now at the threshold of the fourth industrial revolution, what has come to be known as Industry 4.0. It is known that industrialization processes, in the short term, bring critical problems, as distinctly captured by the concept of 'creative destruction', introduced by the Austrian economist Joseph Schumpeter.[15] From a diachronic perspective, however, industrialization and technological transformation processes would appear to call for a more complex assessment. In other words, if we judge the processes unleashed by the industrial revolutions from a transgenerational perspective, weighing up the costs and benefits would appear to give a positive outcome – over the much longer term, for instance, those societies have significantly increased the living standards of their citizens.

Yet, in this context, the climate issue serves to remind us that all that is only a part of the picture. The other part, in fact, concerns changes to the climate caused by human activity. But what are we talking about exactly? What is actually happening to the climate?

The answer to that question can be condensed into a nutshell. Since the turn of the nineteenth century, industrialization processes have required the increasingly massive use of fossil fuels, indispensible to support the spread of electrification processes. Among the most striking side effects of that, we find issues tied to social equality, above all, but also the loss of jobs, especially unskilled jobs, as such workers are replaced in many cases by machines, all of which has been widely studied by social scientists. For a long time, the climate issue was not considered a problem, ultimately because it took many, many decades for the consequences tied to the massive use of fossil fuels to emerge clearly. The consequences tied to or provoked by climate change gradually became clear first of all to scientists. Once the findings of their climate studies were reasonably verified, however, a negationist counter-strategy was put into place by certain lobbies, united under the Global Climate Coalition, concerned that nothing substantial should change as a result of climate policies. The economic interests at threat were (and are) too many and too great, and hence the ultimate objective of the climate change deniers was to minimize the impact on public opinion of the evidence emerging from scientific research.

Let us look at some dates. In 1965, the then US president Lyndon B. Johnson presented the climate issue to Congress. That means that already back then there was sufficient scientific evidence to suggest that world temperatures were rising and that human activity was a determining factor in that process. The fact is significant because it shows that as early as the 1960s or 1970s climate change was gradually emerging as a collateral effect of the industrialization process across the world. Indeed, what was becoming clear was the idea that anthropogenic climate change could bring harmful effects. In terms of political and public responsibility, we can talk of a before and after the awareness of the anthropogenic roots of climate change.

Today we know that virtually any human activity produces greenhouse gases, from the most basic activities that enable us to live, or live decently, to the most complex industrial processes. The economic development that has brought such widespread well-being and relative affluence also concealed a poisonous seed that has grown to threaten the very survival of the planet.

Knowledge of such a state of affairs is important for two reasons. First, knowledge and awareness of what is happening on the climate front is indispensible to open up room for negotiations to reduce the damage and its fallout. Second, on the moral plane, there is a huge difference between knowing and not knowing. Once the veil of ignorance has been raised, there are two options available to us: to take action or to abstain from action, in the pretence that things can continue as they are. The abstentionist option substantially means steering the future in a direction for which, ultimately, we have good reason to believe that non-being will prevail over being.

But let us get back to the facts. The turning point for climate change research came in 1988, when governments agreed to set up the Intergovernmental Panel on Climate Change (IPCC),[16] a research institution bringing together scientists from all around the world. The IPCC has published its findings in a series of assessment reports that have always stressed two points very clearly: the anthropogenic origin of climate change since the early nineteenth century and the harmful nature of such change. As the IPCC's findings grew, after a few years the deniers adopted a more precise obstructionist strategy.

In 1989, the Global Climate Coalition, made up of oil companies, the United States Chamber of Commerce and various manufacturers' associations, commenced a massive media counteroffensive over the issue, directly attacking the IPCC's work and often not disdaining personal attacks on the panel's members. The main argument pushed by the climate change deniers was simple and fallacious. The point, they claimed, is that to fund such radical action against climate change, scientists needed to present evidence that was 100 per cent certain on the anthropogenic causes of the climate's degeneration. Since the sciences cannot provide such certainty – as is consistent, it should be recalled, with the epistemological structure of scientific knowledge – it makes no sense to promote actions that would lead to a decline in growth and affluence. Faced with the uncertainty of the science, they argued, it is better to stick to the certainty of economic growth. In short, better the devil you know.

The specific argument put forth by the climate change deniers is incompatible with the type of knowledge produced by science. Nevertheless, thanks also to the unscrupulous use of mass media,[17] it generally proved to have a good hold on public opinion as a retort to arguments that attempted to highlight the urgency of climate protection measures. The scientific evidence today largely all points to human activity as one of the main causes driving the harmful effects of climate change, underpinning the consensus that if major corrective action is not taken, the planet is destined towards an ontological reversal, where instead of being prevailing over non-being, as it always has, we may be faced with a period of non-being prevailing over being. In other words, from a diachronic perspective, the most likely outcome is that world temperatures will rise by such a degree as to throw the self-regulation mechanism of the Earth System out of whack, with potentially devastating consequences.

The dual strategy

A fundamental milestone was reached in 1992, when the United Nations Conference on Environment and Development was held in Rio de Janeiro. The organizers hoped to forge an agreement that would reconcile various interests and would enable action to be taken to substantially reduce global greenhouse gas emission levels.[18] From an ethical point of view, it was about striking a smart balance between rights and duties, costs and benefits. It was clear for all to see that the most advanced nations had drawn major economic benefits, as the greatest emissions had come from the industrialization processes of those countries. Processes that had, in turn, brought wealth to the populations that had pursued them. On the other hand, the containment of emissions would hit developing countries most, those that needed to emit greenhouse gases to electrify their industrial processes.

An action strategy was thus outlined, envisaging two stages. During the first stage, choices were to be made to permit emerging economies to complete their industrial development. Those economies needed to grow to bring improvement in living standards for their local populations. Only at that point would stage two begin, where developing nations would be called upon to start capping their emissions. In the meantime, the greatest efforts were to be pursued by rich world countries, those that had drawn the greatest benefits from industrialization processes.

The principle steering the agreements forming the Rio Convention is known as the principle of common but differentiated responsibilities. The inspiration behind the principle is simple and reasonable. Under the model adopted, during the first stage, the greatest sacrifices were to be made by rich countries. They were to commit to reducing emissions more than others, developing the scientific research to spread the use of low-impact energy sources, and fostering technological transfer to poorer countries to enable them to play an active part in international cooperation to combat climate change. While the principle may have been fair in terms of equity and justice between nations, rather different conclusions can be drawn as to its effectiveness, given how much it matters when it comes to policy.

The principle of common but differentiated responsibilities, when left to the concerted application of international cooperation, ultimately failed, in the sense that it was never applied. Although the principle was formally adopted at the end of talks at the Rio conference, the United States and oil producing nations in practice undermined any attempt to apply it concretely, by preventing the identification of precise action objectives and realistic time frames. Their obstructionism soon led to the near-total failure of any serious climate negotiations, as witnessed by another two key dates.

The first is 1997, the year the Kyoto Protocol was signed by 191 countries. It committed its signatories to reducing greenhouse gas emissions by an average 8.65 per cent on 1985 levels, considered the base year for measurements. The emission targets applied to the years 2008 to 2014, but as we know today, they were never achieved. Even in this case, US policy decisions played a major role in determining the failure of the common commitment.

The second key date is 2009, when the Copenhagen climate conference was held, marking what was meant to signal a complete overhaul of global climate policies. Leading the US delegation was Barack Obama, who promised a very different approach to climate change compared to the stance taken by the US presidents who had come before him, in particular George W. Bush. Yet, despite Obama's sensitivity to the issue, the outcome of the Copenhagen conference was once again a failure, demonstrating to the world how the approach adopted for over thirty years to forging climate policy – an approach based on international cooperation and negotiation – had largely failed. A combination of national egoisms and diffidence between states – especially the mistrust harboured by developing nations of advanced economies and the decisions they would make – resulted in the collapse of cooperation policies and a substantial breakdown in talks.

The consequences were those that we find ourselves faced with today. With the joint negotiation process essentially at a dead end, nations have begun pursuing their own policy objectives, largely to little effect. Making it much more difficult to achieve concrete targets and virtually impossible to apply principles of justice on the vaster scale.

The principle of transgenerational equity

It must be reiterated how complex the question of climate change is. Whether we address it from the perspective of the application of principles of justice or discuss the matter of corrective measures aimed at reducing greenhouse gases, the issues all overlap and intertwine inexorably.

There are, in fact, two planes that need to be taken into account by scholars and lawmakers concerned with adverse climate change and its harmful effects.

On the one hand, we have issues tied to the application of the principles of equity and justice among nations, along with the right of human beings to live a happy life – this aspect I will call the 'synchronic plane of justice'. On the other, we have issues concerning intergenerational justice and the right of new generations to come into being – this aspect I will call the 'diachronic plane of justice'. One of the critical problems made all too clear by climate change is that the issue is for all intents and purposes multidimensional. It allows for a plurality of conceptualizations and implies the involvement of a plurality of agents who play some part in the matter, ultimately bearing economic, social, political and cultural implications.

The climate issue straddles both the synchronic and diachronic planes of justice, highlighting not only the urgency with which both those planes need to be addressed but also the pressing need to determine their hierarchy. There are good arguments to demonstrate how the two planes do not overlap perfectly. A significant reduction in poverty in a certain country, for instance, can be achieved by creating greater overall wealth, that is, by intensifying the level of industrialization of society. But, as we have seen, that will have the collateral effect of raising emissions, exacerbating the climate problem for new generations to come. Hence, in such a case, the synchronic and diachronic planes are not coextensive, leaving us with a complex knot of issues that are not easy to untie.

The principle of common but differentiated responsibilities represents the cornerstone on which global climate talks have patiently been constructed. It is underpinned by four pillars: historical responsibility, equity, capability and vulnerability. Equity, capability and vulnerability, as I will explain further on, are all criteria that lie on the synchronic plane of justice. Historical responsibility is the only criterion that grasps the diachronic plane, but here it solely concerns the past. Thus, it is diachronic in an important way, but only partially.

The criterion of historical responsibility is based on statistics that show how some countries have contributed much more heavily to greenhouse gas emissions than others, due to the industrialization processes of their economies. Thus, it would appear reasonable to expect that those countries should assume greater responsibility for reducing emissions. Moreover, the biggest emitters are generally also the richest nations, for which, in terms of equity, it would seem fair that the nations with the greatest historical responsibility for emissions should be the first to tackle the problem of emissions. As such, greater efforts are asked of countries in a better position to bear the economic and social costs of the fight against climate change, while paving the way for poorer countries to actively join the struggle at a future stage.

We have seen how awareness represents a fundamental discriminant. Knowing or not knowing – that is, having or not having the scientific data on which to base social and political decisions – is a fundamental element on which to build judgement, including the judgement of historical responsibility. There are good reasons, for instance, for us to attribute specific responsibility to countries that have proved to be the biggest greenhouse gas emitters starting from when science is able to provide data with certainty. As of that historical period, we can talk of direct responsibility because, quite clearly, the weight of responsibility becomes significantly greater when there is awareness.

As concerns the principle of capability, the idea is that the nations that have benefited the most from emissions are also those that have the most sophisticated technological knowledge, and hence the best capability in terms of knowledge and development of relevant technologies. Even in this case, it would seem fair to assume that those same nations are best equipped to engineer innovative solutions to climate change.

Finally, there is the principle of vulnerability. It is widely known that the poorest nations are also those most exposed to bearing the brunt of the adverse consequences of climate change. That is true for various reasons. The main one is that poor countries generally do not have much in the way of funds to invest in efforts to combat climate change directly or to finance measures to mitigate the effects of climate change. In general, such countries are unable to invest sufficiently in developing high-level scientific research and instead need funding to import technology from technologically advanced nations.

All the criteria we have mentioned tie into, and in some way depend on, the criterion of historical responsibility, on which they ultimately are founded. A criterion that steers us to examine historical responsibility can be expected to focus specific attention on what was done – consciously or unconsciously – in the past, thus offering a diachronic perspective that looks primarily to the past. Diachrony, however, means considering time in all its extension, that is, without neglecting the future. In the case at hand, the future is particularly important because it constitutes the dimension in which the metaphysical criterion of being prevailing over non-being is at most serious risk.

As such, I propose supplementing the criterion of historical responsibility with a complementary notion that I shall call the criterion of 'transgenerational responsibility'. The criterion of transgenerational responsibility is founded on a series of premisses:

1. Being is generally better than non-being.
2. There is a transgenerational bond that ties generations to each other, entailing rights and duties within the transgenerational sphere.
3. Transgenerational actions have a peculiar structure, entailing cooperation between generations for a certain action to be accomplished.
4. Social actions of a transgenerational nature must respect the transgenerational bond and be committed to steering the future in ways that will not prejudice or penalize future generations.

Climate change is driven by actions whose transgenerational structure was revealed as of a certain historical era, when the anthropogenic nature of adverse changes to the climate became evident. As we have seen, transgenerational actions imply a duty, at the very least, to steer the future in such a way as not to prejudice the right of future generations to come into existence. The principle of transgenerational responsibility requires that the criterion of vulnerability should be extended to future generations, and not just to the world's poor. If the principle of being prevailing over non-being is reasonably at risk, any prioritization required between defending the interests of poor populations and defending the existence of future generations must necessarily take into account such a risk, which is absolute in nature.

The principle of transgenerational responsibility is exposed to the same type of objection that is often raised against the general containment strategy pursued in addressing climate change, and to ethical principles suggesting the need to reconcile the interests of generations living in the here and now and those of generations yet to be born. The main argument reconciling a certain reasonableness and humanity claims that the need to defend the rights of people living in extreme poverty would appear to prevail, in terms of urgency, over the need to defend the rights of people who do not suffer because they have yet to come into existence. Diminishing the amount of suffering would appear ethically preferable to preventing a suffering that has yet to exist because the sufferers have yet to exist.

Nevertheless, we have seen how the principle of transgenerational responsibility points to a different perspective from which to address the matter, by shifting the emphasis onto two specific elements. First, there is the fact that future generations have the right to exist, assuming as a moral principle that being is generally better than non-being. Second, they have the right to exist because future generations represent a necessary premiss for transgenerational social actions. Without future generations, transgenerational actions, in the majority of cases, could not be brought to complete fulfilment. In other words, they would run the rather serious risk of resembling untenable promises. Third, the transgenerational perspective would imply a certain political stance in relation to the world's poorer nations, which as we have seen, are those that struggle most in finding the right resources to mitigate the effects of climate change. In other words, it is necessary that rich countries commit to transferring technology and knowledge to poor countries, as such transfer would help promote the technological and social development of those nations, thereby lowering poverty through greater economic development.

In its minimal form, the principle of transgenerational responsibility obliges us to accept the rights of future generations to come into being on the basis of two arguments: firstly, that being is better than non-being; and secondly, that future generations are fictional entities whose assumption, by the generations that precede them, enables transgenerational social actions to be brought to complete fulfilment. Such actions are crucial for societies to expand over time, enabling human life to achieve greater complexity and accomplishment. It can be argued, therefore, that the principle of transgenerational responsibility weakly binds each generation in relation to the future. That is to say, it does not commit present generations to offering future generations their same rights and living standards, but it does commit them to guaranteeing future generations the right to come into being.

It makes sense here to ask whether a minimal bond of this kind satisfies us fully and is sufficient to underpin a more general idea of transgenerational justice. In general, I believe the answer is 'No.'[19] Nevertheless, within the restricted scope of the climate issue, recognition of the validity of the principle of transgenerational equity, together with the other criteria that underpin the principle of common responsibilities, enables concrete steps forward to be made towards the primary objective that is the preservation of the planet and its biodiversity.

On the other hand, on a more general level, we have seen how natural it is for social agents – ultimately all of us – to adopt the concept of future generations whenever it is decided to commit to long-term actions that require the commitment of future generations to be brought to term. Thus, for example, if a certain generation, let's say x, expects that other generations should assume the burden of paying the public debt that it has contracted to help lower the level of poverty in society and promote the industrial development of the country in which x lives and future generations will live – actions that, as we now know all too well, will have the collateral effect of emitting harmful greenhouse gases into the atmosphere – then in doing so x must acknowledge the right of those future generations to exist and accept the duty of guaranteeing that such a right can be upheld.

In short, the metaphysical structure of transgenerational social actions, the use that social agents generally make of the concept of future generations in pursuing transgenerational actions and the centrality of the future for a social reality that can offer the possibility of achieving a fuller human dimension, all constitute good reasons to argue that present generations – given that they can and that it is part of the social structure they have constructed – should accept a binding commitment towards the future, doing all that they can to ensure that future generations have the possibility of existing. It is not a gift we offer to those who will come after us, but an obligation that is to be fulfilled, having accepted it.

Such a framework opens up the tricky question to be addressed of how to apply the principle of transgenerational responsibility on the practical plane, and in particular within the context of our democracies. In the current debate, there are, I believe, two overriding issues that call for urgent attention. The first is the general lack of public awareness of the obligation that every generation has towards the future. Yet, it is an obligation that we accept whenever we expect that future generations will commit to the task of fulfilling what we want them to fulfil. Given the general facility with which we assume future generations will do what we need them to do (thus attributing them duties), it is unclear why we should not grant them corresponding rights.

The second issue is no less important and concerns the intrinsic difficulty that democracies face in dealing with the future in ways that are not exclusively parasitic. I believe there are good arguments to be made in support of the idea that if we expand our principles of justice to systematically encompass new generations, we will be forced to profoundly and carefully rethink the very idea and the mechanisms underpinning our democracies. That is for an ultimately quite simple reason. Democracy is a form of government based on the sovereignty of the people, which guarantees each citizen the right to participate on an equal basis in the exercise of public power. In other words, it is a form of government based on the creation and preservation of consensus, specifically the consensus of citizens represented within the democracy. That means that those who have no access to representation – because they are too young, or because they do not have the right to vote, or because they have yet to be born – have no right to be represented, and indeed they are not. That is a major short circuit in the system. Such an impasse risks seriously undermining the survival of our societies, which are already showing cracks caused by their substantial inability to steer the future by taking serious responsibility for it.

Evidently, that is another chapter of the story, complementing what we have explored so far.

Notes

Chapter 1

1. Arendt (1978).
2. The objective of this book falls squarely within the objective of social philosophy, as outlined by Ferrara (2002: 422, 427): 'How can post-traditional societies, no longer cemented by a homogenous horizon of shared meanings, avoid the fate of disintegrating in a kind of ceaseless confrontation that gradually reverts back to the war of all against all?'
3. Ferrara (2002: 427, emphases in the original).
4. Hardin (1968).
5. Spinoza (2000: 235) and Nietzsche (1918). See Spinoza (2000: III, Prop. VI–VII) and Nietzsche (1918). Spinoza writes: 'Most of those who have written about the emotions and about the manner of living of human beings give the impression that they are discussing things that are outside of nature rather than natural things that follow the common laws of nature. In fact, they seem to conceive man in nature as an empire within an empire. […] Here is my reasoning. Nothing happens in nature which can be regarded as nature's fault. Nature is always the same, and everywhere there is one and the same virtue in it, one and the same power of action. That is, the laws rules of nature by which all things happen and change from one form to another are always and everywhere the same, and therefore there must also be one and the same method of reasoning for understanding the nature of anything whatever, namely, through the universal laws and rules of nature' (Spinoza 2000: Part III, Preface; 2018: Part III, Preface).
6. Some theorists of artificial intelligence hold that in the long run immortality will indeed be within the reach of humans, thanks to the creation of an artificial body to which the human brain can be connected. See, for example, Moravec (1988, 1999).
7. Seow (1997: part 1.A. vv. 4–5).
8. See, for example, Gilbert (2014: 58–80), Jaspers (1965) and Lewis (1948).

9. For an approach to questions of transgenerationality grounded in the priority of the collective over the individual, see Stiegler (2014: 17–20).
10. Freud (1953: 23:29).
11. Jung (1972).
12. Searle (1995, 2010).
13. Schützenberger (1998).
14. Searle (1995: 26–27, 37).
15. It is precisely in these terms that Searle explains how skills associated with certain practices are passed on from individual to individual, and from generation to generation through transgenerationality. For his considerations on how primates use sticks as a tool to get bananas that are out of their reach, see Searle (2015: 40).
16. Many of the thoughts in this book are ideally linked to the work of Avenar de-Shalit (1995), who has addressed the issue of transgenerationality with a preference for the ethical-moral perspective. We will advance a series of metaphysical hypotheses with the conviction that a metaphysical foundation can only provide a firmer basis for investigating practical philosophies.
17. For an overview of the literature on the transgenerational transmission of trauma, see Leon Anisfeld and Richards (2000), Grimbert (2008), Schwab (2009) and Assmann and Shortt (2011: 17–33).
18. Quoted in Schützenberger (1998: 131).
19. Spiegelman (2003: 15–16, emphases and ellipses in the original).
20. Leon Anisfeld and Richards (2000: 303).
21. Plato (1930: bk I, 330).
22. The matter itself was raised by Thomas Jefferson in a letter to John Taylor dated 28 May 1816: 'Funding I consider as limited, rightfully, to a redemption of the debt within the lives of a majority of the generation contracting it; every generation coming equally, by the laws of the creator of the world, to the free possession of the earth he made for their subsistence, unencumbered by their predecessors, who, like them, were but tenants for life [...] And I sincerely believe [...] that the principle of spending money to be paid by the posterity, under the name of funding, is but swindling futurity on a large scale.'
23. On these issues, see the documents produced by the Intergovernmental Panel on Climate Change (IPCC), the international body tasked with assessing the work of the sciences involved in monitoring climate change (IPCC 2021).
24. Brown Weiss (1988).
25. World Commission on Environment and Development (1987: 43).
26. See Dobson (1999), Tremmel (2006) and Gündling (1990).

27 Parfit (1982). Here we look at the version of the argument as put forth by Parfit, however, it should be stated that the paradox was also formulated independently by Adams (1979: 57) and Schwartz ('Obligations to Posterity', in Sikora and Barry 1978).
28 For a general discussion of positions that fall under the name of the 'non-identity problem' or 'future individual paradox', see Tremmel (2009: 50–52).
29 D'Amato (1990).
30 D'Amato (1990: 194).
31 Gündling (1990: 210).
32 See, for example, Arendt (1958) and Weil (1953). Arendt, in particular, is critical of the idea that free time, or time freed from labour and work, is used by humans for anything other than consumption.
33 See the paper 'The Future of the Job' presented at the World Economic Forum, from which it emerged how in forthcoming years, demographic factors and changes caused in various ways by new technologies will lead to an overall loss of around seven million jobs, while creating around two million new jobs. The estimated net outcome, therefore, prospects a major and generalized loss of jobs, while the types of jobs available on the market are forecast to change.
34 Ferraris (2015).
35 Dixon (2003).
36 On the transformation of the world of work in the age of digital transformation, see Toracca and Condello (2019).
37 For a comprehensive and up-to-date overview, see Camboni (2018: 2–26).
38 Tuomela (2013).
39 Giubboni (2012: 530).
40 Scholz (2008: 21–22).
41 Tuomela (2013: 243).
42 Rehg (2007: 7).
43 Tuomela (2013: 241–243).
44 Wiggins (2009: 247, quote at 251).
45 Hume (2007).
46 Barker et al. (1980).
47 Weil (1981).

Chapter 2

1 In this regard, see Nussbaum (2018).
2 On the centrality of the notion of recognition for social philosophy, see also Ferrara (2002: 431).

3   Richard H. Thaler, an American economist and winner of the 2017 Nobel Prize for his contribution to behavioural economics, proposes deconstructing the idea in the field of economics. On this matter, see Thaler (2018).
4   Wolff (1970: 78, my emphasis).
5   Wolff (1970: 70).
6   Machiavelli (2013: § xvii).
7   Vico (2020: §367).
8   Vico (2020).
9   Vico (2020: 141).
10 Vico (2020).
11 See, for example, Hobbes in *De cive*: 'Let us return again to the state of nature, and consider men as if but even now sprung out of the earth, and suddainly (like mushrooms) come to full maturity without all kind of engagement to each other' (Hobbes 1983: VIII, I).
12 Vico (2020: §239).
13 Vico (2020: 341).
14 Hobbes (1998: The Epistle Dedicatory).
15 Hobbes (1983: 34).
16 Aristotle (2013: 1252 a).
17 Hobbes (1983: III, XIII).
18 Along the same lines, see Machiavelli (2013: § viii).
19 See Hobbes (1983: 44) and *Leviathan*: 'Againe, men have no pleasure (but on the contrary a great deale of griefe) in keeping company, where there is no power able to over-awe them all' (Hobbes 1881: I, § XIII, p. 162).
20 Hobbes (1983: II, VI).
21 Ibid., emphases in the original.
22 Hobbes (1983: VIII).
23 Schopenhauer et al. (2010: book two, § 20).
24 Schopenhauer et al. (2010: book two, § 20).
25 See also the reading offered by Hobbes (2014: ch. VI).
26 Spinoza (2018: III, pp. 6–7).
27 Nietzsche (1967: § 630).
28 Nietzsche (1967: § 636, my emphasis).
29 Spinoza (2018: III, p. 3).
30 Spinoza (2018: III, p. 9, emphasis in the original).
31 Spinoza (2018: III, p. 56).
32 Spinoza (2018: III, p. 18s2, emphases in the original).

33 'The excluded party spoils the other's possession, by introducing his excluded being-for-himself into it, his [sense of] "mine." He ruins something in it, annihilating [i.e. negating] it as desire, in order to give himself his self-feeling [*Selbstgefühl*] – yet not his empty self-feeling, but rather positing his own Self in another, in the knowing of another' (Hegel and Rauch 1983: 115).
34 Honneth (1995: 16).
35 'In recognition [*Anerkennen*], the Self ceases to be this individual; it exists by right in recognition, i.e., no longer [immersed] in its immediate existence. The one who is recognized is recognized as immediately counting as such [*geltend*], through his *being* – but this being is itself generated from the concept; it is recognized being [*anerkanntes Seyn*]. Man is necessarily recognized and necessarily gives recognition. This necessity is his own, not that of our thinking in contrast to the content. As recognizing, man is himself the movement [of recognition], and this movement itself is what negates [*hebt auf*] his natural state: he is recognition' (Hegel and Rauch 1983: 111, emphasis in the original).
36 Honneth (2003: 54–55).
37 Mead (2009: 152 ss.).
38 Mead (2009: 161).
39 Ibid.
40 Mead (2009: 210).
41 Dickson et al. (2018).
42 See Kalmakis and Chandler (2015).
43 See, for example, Santavirta, Santavirta and Gilman (2018) and Bohacek and Mansuy (2015).

Chapter 3

1 On this subject, cf. Forsyth (2007), Verma (2006).
2 Kant (1991: 177, emphasis in the original).
3 Kant (1991: 44, emphases in the original).
4 Kant (1991: 42–43).
5 Kant (1991: 44).
6 Dilthey (1990).
7 On these matters, see also Pinder (1928: ch. VII).
8 Mannheim (1952: 286).
9 Mannheim (1952: 255).

10 Mannheim (1952: 257).
11 Brock and Everett (2015).
12 Thomasson (1999: 139–145).
13 See Margolis and Laurence (2007: 52–73).
14 Thomasson (2003: 580–609).
15 Besides Thomasson in the field of metaphysics, the same argument is put forth in the architectural sphere by Armando and Durbiano (2017).
16 Tolstoy (2010: bk 1, pt 1, ch. 2).
17 Hume (2018: 5103).
18 For a more in-depth discussion of these issues, see Andina (2017).
19 The Rumor government was the twenty-third government of the Italian Republic, the second of the fifth legislature.
20 Kant (1991: 41–53).
21 Kant (1991: 42–43).
22 Kant (1991: 44).
23 See, for example, the classic works of Anscombe (1957) and Davidson (2001).
24 Frankfurt (1978: 157–162).
25 Danto (1973).
26 See, especially, Searle (1995, 2010). For a weaker version of collective intentionality, to which we will refer extensively in our discussion, see Tuomela (2002).
27 Searle (1995: 23–26).
28 Tuomela (2002: 19).
29 Tuomela (2002: 20).
30 On these issues, see Anscombe (1957).
31 For an analysis of the differences between loyalty and solidarity, see Kolers (2016: 44 ss.).
32 Kolers (2016: 29, 52 ss.).
33 On the role of institutions in preserving social and political well-being, see Acemoglu and Robinson (2012).
34 Bagnoli (2019).

Chapter 4

1 Schumpeter (2001).
2 Acemoglu and Robinson (2012).
3 INPS (2017).

4   For the full text of the decree, see Comune di Jesi (1974).
5   For an interesting dynamic comparison of the economic trends of the world's major industrialized nations between 1960 and 2017, see World GDP by Country in the video by WawamuStats (2018).
6   See Jonas (1979). Jonas addresses the question of the importance of the future in structuring social models, focusing above all on the role and potential of technology. His underlying theory is substantially that since technological development has accelerated the possibility of human intervention in nature considerably, and since technological development over the last century has proved capable, as never before, of altering the deeper equilibria of nature, it is imperative that humans take responsibility for making predictions that take up even the most adverse consequences. For Jonas, therefore, building the social world means first and foremost taking responsibility for the consequences of social decisions and actions, and hence reckoning with the future.
7   See, for example, the observations of Van Parijs (1998: 294–299).
8   In relation to some possible corrective measures, for an initial discussion, see Van Parijs (1998: 301–308).
9   The distinction between extractive economies and inclusive economies is outlined in detail by Acemoglu and Robinson (2012: 149–160).
10 Di Paola (2015: 107).
11 United Nations (1992).
12 A comparable premiss, in a similar context, is defended by Jonas (1979).
13 As we have already seen, the paradox outlined by Derek Parfit (1982) merits close consideration. It has long been held up as an argument against the idea that it makes sense to protect future generations, on the grounds that, in a nutshell, climate action would alter the climatic and environmental conditions to which life generation processes are extremely sensitive. Thus, it could turn out that the generations we seek to protect may never see the light, in the sense that other individuals may be born in place of those that would be born under certain conditions. If that is the case, then any action taken to protect future generations may provoke more serious damage than what we are trying to avoid. Parfit's position is quite clearly a deflationist one, in that it reduces future generations to the individuals that make them up. In metaphysical terms, however, that is just one option available to us. Another option is to conceptualize future generations differently, by treating them, for example, as entities not reducible to the individuals that make them up, but as fictional entities with the characteristic of passing from potentiality to actuality. Assuming that the argument of being

prevailing over non-being, as a general principle, transcends the specificity of the single individual, I believe that treating future generations as abstract artefacts with the characteristic of passing from potentiality to actuality enables us to avoid the problem posed by Parfit – a problem that, curiously, in seeking to protect the single individual endorses a position that would risk destroying the human race itself, resulting in exactly what Parfit seeks to prevent, namely, the destruction of the single individual.

14 For an in-depth discussion of the social aspects of the first Industrial Revolution, see Thompson (1968).
15 Schumpeter (2001).
16 The IPCC's assessment reports, along with more recent studies and considerations on the future of climate change, can be found on its website (IPCC n.d.).
17 On this, see Anderson (2011); on the question of post-truth in the climate debate, see Condello and Andina (2019).
18 For a detailed look at the history of the social and political events that led to the explosion of the climate issue, see Di Paola (2015: 43–50).
19 For a more in-depth discussion of these issues, I take the liberty of referring readers to Condello and Andina (2019).

Bibliography

Acemoglu, Daron, and James A. Robinson. 2012. *Why Nations Fail: The Origins of Power, Prosperity, and Poverty*. New York: Crown Publishing Group.

Adams, Robert Merrihew. 1979. 'Existence, Self-Interest, and the Problem of Evil'. *Noûs* 13 (1): 53–65. doi: 10.2307/2214795.

Anderson, Elizabeth. 2011. 'Democracy, Public Policy, and Lay Assessments of Scientific Testimony'. *Episteme* 8 (2): 144–164. doi: 10.3366/epi.2011.0013.

Andina, Tiziana. 2017. *What Is Art?: The Question of Definition Reloaded*. Brill Research Perspectives in Art and Law. Leiden: Brill.

Anscombe, G.E.M. 1957. *Intention*. Ithaca, NY: Cornell University Press.

Arendt, Hannah. 1958. *The Human Condition, Charles R. Walgreen Foundation Lectures*. Chicago: University of Chicago Press.

Arendt, Hannah. 1978. *The Life of the Mind*. 1st edn. 2 vols. New York: Harcourt Brace Jovanovich.

Aristotle. 2013. *Aristotle's Politics*. 2nd edn. Chicago: University of Chicago Press.

Armando, Alessandro, and Giovanni Durbiano. 2017. *Teoria del progetto architettonico. Dai disegni agli effetti*. Rome: Carocci.

Assmann, Aleida, and Linda Shortt. 2011. *Memory and Political Change*. Basingstoke, UK: Palgrave Macmillan.

Bagnoli, Carla. 2019. *Teoria della Responsibilità*. Bologna: Il Mulino.

Barker, Ernest, John Locke, David Hume and Jean-Jacques Rousseau. 1980. *Social Contract: Essays by Locke, Hume, and Rousseau*. Westport, CT: Greenwood Press.

Bohacek, Johannes, and Isabelle M. Mansuy. 2015. 'Molecular Insights into Transgenerational Non-genetic Inheritance of Acquired Behaviours'. *Nature Reviews Genetics* 16: 641–652. doi: 10.1038/nrg3964.

Brock, Stuart, and Anthony Everett. 2015. *Fictional Objects*. Oxford: Oxford University Press.

Camboni, Francesco. 2018. 'La solidarietà come concetto filosofico'. *Bilioteca della libertà* 53 (221) (January–April): 3–26. doi: 10.23827/BDL_2018_1_5.

Comune di Jesi. 1974. 'D.P.R. 29 dicembre 1973, n. 1092 Approvazione del testo unico delle norme sul trattamento di quiescenza dei dipendenti civili e militari dello Stato'. 9 May. Available online: http://www.comune.jesi.an.it/MV/leggi/dpr1092-73.htm (accessed 30 July 2021).

Condello, Angela, and Tiziana Andina, eds. 2019. *Post-Truth, Philosophy and Law*. Law and Politics: Continental Perspectives series. Abingdon, UK: Routledge.

D'Amato, Anthony. 1990. 'Do We Owe a Duty to Future Generations to Preserve the Global Environment?', *American Journal of International Law* 84 (1): 190–198. doi: 10.2307/2203019.

Danto, Arthur C. 1973. *Analytical Philosophy of Action*. Cambridge: Cambridge University Press.

Davidson, Donald. 2001. *Essays on Actions and Events*. 2nd edn. Oxford: Clarendon Press.

De-Shalit, Avner. 1995. *Why Posterity Matters: Environmental Policies and Future Generations*. Environmental Philosophies series. London: Routledge.

Di Paola, Marcello. 2015. *Cambiamento climatico. Una piccola introduzione*. Rome: Luiss University Press.

Dickson, David A., Jessica K. Paulus, Virginia Mensah, Janis Lem, Lorena Saavedra-Rodriguez, Adrienne Gentry, Kelly Pagidas and Larry A. Feig. 2018. 'Reduced Levels of miRNAs 449 and 34 in Sperm of Mice and Men Exposed to Early Life Stress'. *Translational Psychiatry* 8 (1): 101. doi: 10.1038/s41398-018-0146-2.

Dilthey, Wilhelm. 1990. *Über das Studium der Geschichte der Wissenschaften vom Menschen, der Gesellschaft und dem Staat (1875)*, vol. 5, *Die geistige Welt*. Göttingen: Vandenhoeck & Ruprecht.

Dixon, Sylvia. 2003. 'Implications of Population Ageing for the Labour Market'. *Labour Market Trends* 111 (2): 67–76.

Dobson, Andrew. 1999. *Fairness and Futurity: Essays on Environmental Sustainability and Social Justice*. Oxford: Oxford University Press.

Ferrara, Alessandro. 2002. 'The Idea of a Social Philosophy'. *Constellations* 9 (3): 419–435. doi: 10.1111/1467-8675.00291.

Forsyth, Miranda. 2007. 'A Typology of Relationships between State and Non-State Justice Systems', *The Journal of Legal Pluralism and Unofficial Law*, vol. 39 n. 56, pp. 67–112.

Ferraris, Maurizio. 2015. *Mobilitazione totale*. Rome: Laterza.

Frankfurt, Harry G. 1978. 'The Problem of Action'. *American Philosophical Quarterly* 15 (2): 157–162.

Freud, Sigmund. 1953. *The Standard Edition of the Complete Psychological Works of Sigmund Freud*. 24 vols. London: Hogarth Press.

Gilbert, Margaret. 2014. *Joint Commitment: How We Make the Social World*. New York: Oxford University Press.

Giubboni, Stefano. 2012. 'Solidarietà'. *Politica del diritto* 43 (4): 525–553.

Grimbert, Philippe. 2008. *Secret*. London: Portobello Books.

Gündling, Lothar. 1990. 'Our Responsibility to Future Generations'. *American Journal of International Law* 84 (1): 207–212. doi: 10.2307/2203021.

Hardin, Garrett. 1968. 'The Tragedy of the Commons'. *Science* 162 (3859): 1243–1248. doi: 10.1126/science.162.3859.1243.

Hegel, G.W.F., and L. Rauch. 1983. *Hegel and the Human Spirit: A Translation of the Jena Lectures on the Philosophy of Spirit (1805-6) with Commentary*. Detroit, MI: Wayne State University Press.

Hobbes, Thomas. 1881. *Leviathan*. Oxford: J. Thornton.

Hobbes, Thomas. 1983. *De cive: the English version entitled, in the first edition, Philosophicall rudiments concerning government and society, The Clarendon edition of the philosophical works of Thomas Hobbes*. Edited by Howard Warrender. Oxford: Clarendon Press.

Hobbes, Thomas. 1998. *On the Citizen*. Translated by De Cive. New York: Cambridge University Press. Translated by T. Magri as *Elementi filosofici sul cittadino*. Rome: Rubettino, 2005.

Hobbes, Thomas. 2014. *Leviathan*. Oxford: Clarendon Press. Translated by R. Giammanco as *Il leviatano*. Turin: UTET, 1955.

Honneth, Axel. 1995. *The Struggle for Recognition: The Moral Grammar of Social Conflicts*. 1st edn. Studies in Contemporary German Social Thought series. Cambridge, MA: MIT Press.

Honneth, Axel. 2003. *Kampf um Anerkennung*. Berlin: Suhrkamp. Translated by C. Sandrelli as *Lotta per il riconoscimeno*. Milan: Il saggiatore, 2002.

Hume, David. 2007. *A Treatise of Human Nature: A Critical Edition*. 2 vols. Oxford: Clarendon Press.

Hume, David. 2018. *David Hume on Morals, Politics, and Society*. Edited by Angela Coventry and Andrew Valls. New Haven, CT: Yale University Press.

INPS. 2017. 'La Storia'. 3 April. Available online: https://www.inps.it/nuovoportaleinps/default.aspx?sPathID=%3b0%3b51646%3b&lastMenu=51646&iMenu=11&p4=2 (accessed 30 July 2021).

Intergovernmental Panel on Climate Change (IPCC). 2021. Available online: http://www.ipcc.ch (accessed 30 July 2021).

Intergovernmental Panel on Climate Change (IPCC). n.d. 'About the IPCC'. Available online: https://www.ipcc.ch/about/ (accessed 30 July 2021).

Jaspers, Karl. 1965. *The Question of German Guilt*. New York: Fordham University Press.

Jonas, Hans. 1979. *Das Prinzip Verantwortung: Versuch einer Ethik für die technologische Zivilisation*. 1st edn. Frankfurt am Main: Insel-Verlag. Translated by P. Portinaro as *Principio responsabilità*. Turin: Einaudi, 2009.

Jung, C.G. 1972. *Two Essays on Analytical Psychology*. 2nd edn. *The Collected Works of C G Jung*. Princeton, NJ: Princeton University Press.

Kalmakis, Karen A., and Genevieve E. Chandler. 2015. 'Health Consequences of Adverse Childhood Experiences: A Systematic Review'. *Journal of the American Association of Nurse Practitioners* 27 (8): 457–465. doi: 10.1002/2327-6924.12215.

Kant, Immanuel. 1991. *Kant: Political Writings*. Edited by Hans Siegbert Reiss. 2nd enlarged edn. Cambridge Texts in the History of Political Thought series. Cambridge: Cambridge University Press.

Kolers, Avery. 2016. *A Moral Theory of Solidarity*. Oxford: Oxford University Press.

Leon Anisfeld, D.S.W., and Arnold D. Richards. 2000. 'The Replacement Child: Variations on a Theme in History and Psychoanalysis.' *Psychoanalytic Study of the Child* 55: 301–318.

Lewis, H.D. 1948. 'Collective Responsibility'. *Philosophy* 23 (84): 3–18.

Machiavelli, Niccolò. 2013. *Il Principe*. Milan: Feltrinelli Editore.

Mannheim, Karl. 1952. *Essays on the Sociology of Knowledge*. London: Routledge & K. Paul. Translated by M. Gagliardi and T. Souvan as *Sociologia della conoscenza*. Bologna: Il Mulino, 2000.

Margolis, Eric, and Stephen Laurence. 2007. *Creations of the Mind: Theories of Artifacts and Their Representation*. Oxford: Clarendon Press.

Mead, George Herbert. 2009. *Mind, Self, and Society: From the Standpoint of a Social Behaviorist*. Chicago: University of Chicago Press.

Moravec, Hans P. 1988. *Mind Children: The Future of Robot and Human Intelligence*. Cambridge, MA: Harvard University Press.

Moravec, Hans P. 1999. *Robot: Mere Machine to Transcendent Mind*. New York: Oxford University Press.

Nietzsche, Friedrich Wilhelm. 1918. *The Genealogy of Morals*. Translated by Horace Barnett Samuel. The Modern Library of the World's Best Books series. New York: Boni and Liveright.

Nietzsche, Friedrich Wilhelm. 1967. *The Will to Power*. Translated by Walter Arnold Kaufmann and R.J. Hollingdale. New York: Random House. Translated by M. Ferraris as *Volontà di potenza*. Milan: Bompiani, 2001.

Nussbaum, M.C. 2018. *The Monarchy of Fear: A Philosopher Looks at Our Political Crisis*. New York: Simon & Schuster.

Parfit, Derek. 1982. 'Future Generations: Further Problems'. *Philosophy & Public Affairs* 11 (2): 113–172.

Pinder, Wilhelm. 1928. 'Das Problem der Generation in der Kunstgeschichte Europas'. *Annalen der Philosophie Und Philosophischen Kritik* 7: 122.

Plato. 1930. *The Republic*. Translated by Paul Shorey. Cambridge, MA: Harvard University Press.

Rehg, William. 2007. 'Solidarity and the Common Good: An Analytic Framework'. *Journal of Social Philosophy* 38 (1): 7–21. doi: doi:10.1111/j.1467-9833.2007.00363.x.

Santavirta Torsten, Nina Santavirta and Stephen E. Gilman. 2018. 'Association of the World War II Finnish Evacuation of Children with Psychiatric Hospitalization in the Next Generation'. *JAMA Psychiatry* 75 (1): 21–27. doi: doi:10.1001/jamapsychiatry.2017.3511.

Scholz, Sally J. 2008. *Political Solidarity*. University Park: Penn State University Press.

Schopenhauer, Arthur, Judith Norman, Alistair Welchman and Christopher Janaway. 2010. *The World as Will and Representation*. The Cambridge Edition of the Works of Schopenhauer. Cambridge: Cambridge University Press.

Schumpeter, Joseph A. 2001. *Capitalismo, socialismo e democrazia*. Translated by E. Zuffi. Milan: Etas.

Schützenberger, Anne Ancelin. 1998. *The Ancestor Syndrome: Transgenerational Psychotherapy and the Hidden Links in the Family Tree*. London: Routledge.

Schwab, G. 2009. 'Replacement Children: The Transgenerational Transmission of Traumatic Loss'. *American Imago* 66 (3): 277–310.

Searle, John R. 1995. *The Construction of Social Reality*. New York: Free Press.

Searle, John R. 2010. *Making the Social World: The Structure of Human Civilization*. Oxford: Oxford University Press.

Searle, John R. 2015. *Seeing Things as They Are: A Theory of Perception*. Oxford: Oxford University Press.

Seow, Choon-Leong. 1997. *Ecclesiastes: A New Translation with Introduction and Commentary*. New Brunswick, NJ: Doubleday.

Sikora, Richard I., and Brian Barry. 1978. *Obligations to Future Generations*. Philadelphia: Temple University Press.

Spiegelman, Art. 2003. *Complete Maus*. London: Penguin.

Spinoza, Benedictus de. 2000. *Ethics*. Edited and translated by G.H.R. Parkinson. Oxford Philosophical Texts series. Oxford: Oxford University Press.

Spinoza, Benedictus de. 2018. *Ethics*. Edited by Matthew J. Kisner. Cambridge Texts in the History of Philosophy series. New York: Cambridge University Press.

Stiegler, Bernard. 2014. *Prendersi cura. Della gioventù e delle generazioni*. Edited and translated by Paolo Vignola. Naples: Orthotes.

Thaler, Richard H. 2018. *Misbehaving. La nascita della economia comportamentale*. Translated by Giuseppe Barile. Turin: Einaudi.

Thomasson, Amie L. 1999. *Fiction and Metaphysics*. Cambridge Studies in Philosophy series. Cambridge: Cambridge University Press.

Thomasson, Amie L. 2003. 'Realism and Human Kinds'. *Philosophy and Phenomenological Research* 67 (3): 580–609.

Thompson, E.P. 1968. *The Making of the English Working Class*. New edn. Pelican Books, A1000. Harmondsworth, UK: Penguin.

Tolstoy, Leo. 2010. *War and Peace*. Translated with notes by Louise and Aylmer Maude. Revised and edited with an introduction by Amy Mandelker. Oxford: Oxford University Press.

Toracca, Tiziano, and Angela Condello, eds. 2019. *Law, Labour and the Humanities*. London: Routledge.

Tremmel, Jörg. 2006. *Handbook of Intergenerational Justice*. Cheltenham, UK: Edward Elgar.

Tremmel, Jörg. 2009. *A Theory of Intergenerational Justice*. London: Taylor & Francis Group.

Tuomela, Raimo. 2002. *The Philosophy of Social Practices: A Collective Acceptance View*. Cambridge: Cambridge University Press.

Tuomela, Raimo. 2013. *Social Ontology: Collective Intentionality and Group Agents*. New York: Oxford University Press.

United Nations. 1992. Framework Convention on Climate Change. Available online: https://unfccc.int/resource/docs/convkp/conveng.pdf (accessed 30 July 2021).

Van Parijs, Philippe. 1998. 'The Disfranchisement of the Elderly, and Other Attempts to Secure Intergenerational Justice'. *Philosophy & Public Affairs* 27 (4): 292–333.

Verma, Vidhu. 2006. 'The State, Democracy and Global Justice', *Economic and Political Weekly*, vol. 41 n. 34, pp. 3728–3735.

Vico, Giambattista. 2020. *The New Science*. Edited and translated by Jason Taylor and Robert C. Miner, introduction by Giuseppe Mazzotta. New Haven, CT: Yale University Press.

WawamuStats. 2018. [Video] 'The World's 10 Biggest Economies by GDP since 1960, Visualized Like a Horserace'. 6 September. Available online: http://digg.com/video/top-10-countries-by-gdp-1960-2017 (accessed 30 July 2021).

Weil, Simone. 1953. *La source grecque*. Paris: Gallimard.

Weil, Simone. 1981. *The Iliad: Or The Poem of Force*. Wallingford, PA: Pendle Hill.

Weiss, Edith Brown. 1988. *In Fairness to Future Generations: International Law, Common Patrimony, and Intergenerational Equity*. Tokyo: United Nations University; Dobbs Ferry, NY: Transnational Publishers.

Wiggins, David. 2009. 'Solidarity and the Root of the Ethical'. *Tijdschrift voor Filosofie* 71 (2): 239–269.

Wolff, R.P. 1970. *In Defense of Anarchism*. Berkeley: University of California Press.

World Commission on Environment and Development. 1987. *Our Common Future*. Oxford: Oxford University Press.

Index

Acemoglu, Daron, and James A. Robinson 132
Adams, Robert Merrihew 161
Agreement(s) 16, 28, 97–9, 118, 145, 147, 151
Alighieri, Dante 49–50
Allen, Woody 2, 86, 103
Amato, Giuliano 138
Anderson, Elizabeth 166
Anisfeld, Leon 14
Anscombe, Gertrude Elizabeth Margaret 164
Antingone 7–8
Arendt, Hannah 1, 159, 161
Aristotle 39, 54
Armando, Alessandro, and Giovanni Durbiano 164
Artefacts 88–95, 97, 103
Assmann, Aleida, and Linda Shortt 160

Bagnoli, Carla 164
Barker, Ernest 161
Bohacek, Johannes 163
Brock, Stuart 164
Brown, Weiss Edith 17
Bush, George W. 152

Camboni, Francesco 161
Cervantes, Miguel de 100
Charlemagne 132
Climate Change 4, 17, 129, 145–56
Collective action(s) 27, 109–13, 145
Common good(s) 5–6, 17, 27, 32, 120, 135
Common-sense argument 2, 86–7, 103
Condello, Angela 161, 166
Conflict 6–8, 21–3, 32, 38, 48, 56–8, 148
Contract 37, 43, 54–5, 57–8, 97–8, 133–5

D'Amato, Anthony 19–20
Dalí, Salvador 11–12

Danto, Arthur 108
Darwin, Charles 48
Davidson, Donald 164
Democracies 2, 25, 75, 86, 98, 126, 142–3, 157–8
Di Paola, Marcello 165–6
Dickson, David 64–5
Dilthey, Wilhelm 82–3, 85
Dixon, Sylvia 161
Dobson, Andrew 160

Equality 17, 19, 39–41, 44, 63, 148
Emotion(s) 7, 14, 23–5, 31, 35–7, 40, 45, 50–3, 55, 58, 62–3, 69–70
Environment 6, 17–9, 48, 150
Everett, Anthony 164

Fear 23–5, 33–5, 37–41, 44–7, 49, 52–3, 55, 58, 93
Ferrante, Elena 100
Ferrara, Alessandro 2, 159
Ferraris, Maurizio 161
Fictional 49, 87–8, 92–5, 100, 102–3, 128, 156
Frankfurt, Harry G. 108, 116
Freud, Sigmund 9, 160
Future Generations 1–5, 16–21, 58, 66, 69, 74–8, 81–2, 86–8, 94–103, 118–19, 122–3, 128, 142, 145–6, 155–7

Gilbert, Margaret 159
Giubboni, Stefano 161
Grimbert, Philippe 160
Gündling, Lothar 20, 160–1

Hardin, Garrett 4–6, 159
Hegel, Georg Wilhelm Friedrich 7, 31, 42, 56–60, 62, 64–6, 71, 73–4, 83
Hobbes, Thomas 26, 33, 36–46, 48–9, 51, 54–6, 73

Homer 95
Honneth, Axel 56
Hume, David 28, 97–8

Individualism 26, 29, 33, 54, 56, 78
Intergenerational 2, 18, 21–2, 105, 123–5, 138, 153

Jaspers, Karl 159
Jefferson, Thomas 160
Johnson, Lyndon B. 149
Jonas, Hans 142, 165
Jung, Ernst 9, 160
Justice 15, 33, 70, 76, 98–9, 120–1, 124–6, 128–9, 137–9, 143–4, 151–3, 156, 158

Kalmakis, Karen A., and Genevieve E. Chandler 163
Kant, Immanuel 77–81, 97, 105–7
Kolers, Avery 121, 164

Labour Market 22–3, 129, 136
Laurence, Stephen 164
Lewis, David 159

Machiavelli, Niccolò 33, 54
Mannheim, Karl 83–5
Mansuy, Isabelle M. 163
Manzoni, Alessandro 100
Margolis, Eric 164
Marx, Groucho 2
Marx, Karl 33
Mead, George Herbert 59–64, 74
Metaphysics 34, 52, 59, 70
Moravec, Hans 159

Nietzsche, Friedrich W. 5, 35, 40, 46–51
Nussbaum, Martha C. 161

Obama, Barack 152
Ontology 3, 24–5, 31, 33, 37, 46, 48, 66, 108

Parfit, Derek 18–20
Pinder, Wilhelm 163
Plato 15
Primary Transgenerationality 7–14, 29, 64, 66, 69, 70–2, 74, 80, 83, 105
Public Debt 11, 15–6, 22, 99, 122, 124, 129, 157

Recognition 28, 31, 40, 56–66, 71, 73, 81, 104, 156
Rehg, William 161
Responsibility 1, 21, 26, 32, 71–2, 74, 78, 127–9, 145, 149, 153–8
Richards, Arnold D. 14
Rumor, Mariano 101, 137–8, 142–4, 164

Santavirta, Torsten, Nina Santavirta, and Stephen E. Gilman 163
Scholz, Sally 161
Schopenhauer, Arthur 46–7, 49–51
Schumpeter, Joseph 131, 148
Schützenberger, Anne 10–2, 160
Schwab, Gabriele 160
Schwartz, Thomas 161
Searle, John R. 9–10, 109–10
Sikora, Richard I., and Brian Barry 161
Social Action 3, 7, 20, 66, 103, 113, 127–9, 134, 155–7
Sociality 9, 37–9, 57–8, 63
Solidarity 26–9, 50–1, 120–1, 124–6
Spiegelman, Art 13–14
Spinoza, Benedictus de 5, 47, 51–3, 55, 70
State of Nature 34, 38–41, 44–6, 49, 54–5
Stiegler, Bernard 160

Taylor, John 160
Thaler, Richard 162
Thomasson, Amie 87, 90
Thompson, Edward Palmer 166
Tolstoy, Leo 93, 100
Toracca, Tiziano 161
Trauma 7–8, 11, 14, 65
Tremmel, Jörg Chet 160–61
Trust 41–2, 44, 100, 115–20
Tuomela, Raimo 27–8, 110–12

United States 15, 150–51

van Gogh, Theo 12
van Gogh, Vincent 11–12
Van Parijs, Philippe 165
Vico, Giambattista 34–9, 41–2, 46

Weil, Simone 28
Wiggins, David 28
Wittgenstein, Ludwig 107
Wolff, Robert P. 32–3

www.ingramcontent.com/pod-product-compliance
Lightning Source LLC
Chambersburg PA
CBHW061837300426
44115CB00013B/2416